EUROPEAN EXCURSIONS

My Collection of Solo Adventures While Traveling Throughout Europe

EUROPEAN EXCURSIONS

*My Collection of Solo Adventures
While Traveling Throughout Europe*

By Leroy Martin

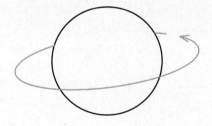

This book is dedicated to
Nevin and Dorcas Martin and family.

There are no foreign lands.
It is the traveler only who is foreign.

–Robert Louis Stevenson

As cold waters to a thirsty soul,
so is good news from a far country.
–Proverbs 25:25

Table of Contents

EUROPEAN EXCURSIONS

*My Collection
of Solo Adventures
While Traveling
Throughout Europe*

The author traveled Spain, France, Italy, Switzerland, Germany, Lithuania, Austria, The Netherlands, Vatican City, Belgium, the UK (London), Norway, Finland, Denmark, Sweden, Slovakia, Hungary, Poland, Czech Republic, and Iceland.

ACKNOWLEDGMENTS

To Andrew. I cannot express adequate gratitude for the selfless dedication which you applied to my second book project. Thank you so much for providing your graphic designing expertise and for sharing your ideas and insight. Without the aid of your visual craftmanship, this book would fail to sufficiently convey my travel experiences in Europe. It is always a pleasure of mine to witness your skilled handiwork.

To Raymond. Thank you for the opportunity to travel to Europe for the duration of several weeks and report on my findings there. It was a beneficial experience which provided me with a glimpse into our Anabaptist history as well as providing an excellent opportunity to become briefly acquainted with other people's cultures and practices. Thank you also for setting aside time to read this book and for producing a foreword. I have developed a great fondness and respect for the written word; thank you for all that you have taught me and continue to teach me regarding the publishing industry. Thanks also for being a great Team Leader.

To Chris. You invested a great deal of your time in my project. The extensiveness and willingness in which you approached this project was much appreciated and highly regarded. Thank you very much for everything you did in helping me shape this book from a mere idea to a product which would occupy the shelves of several bookstores and be introduced to a few mailboxes as well.

To Ivan. You generously gave of your time in printing and binding a few proofs and provided me with insight and suggestions. Thank you for the time and interest which you invested. Additionally, thank you for sharing some of your knowledge regarding accounting.

To Ivan Lee. Thank you for once again combing through a pile of documents which I shared with you. The thorough process in which you scoured the final draft for any errors which might have otherwise eluded my eyes was appreciated. Thank you also for teaching me to appreciate our feathered friends. Birds sure are special creatures, and I have been noticing them more since you joined the *PCBE* team.

To Mervin. Even though typing a few words isn't exactly your cup of tea, I am grateful that you were willing to set aside some of your valuable time to read my draft and then generate—at my behest—a few words regarding your take on my work. Thank you. Additionally, thank you for teaching me everything you know about dogs.

To John. Thank you for the time which you dedicated in providing your thoughts regarding the final draft which I typed for this second book project of mine. The timing was slightly unhandy for you, since you had many projects of your own that you were simultaneously trying to complete, however, you provided me with good feedback. Thank you for teaching me how to avoid burning my food when I am grilling.

To Lavern. Whenever I wanted to quit writing this book—because it would have been easier to do so—you consistently provided much needed encouragement, and helped me to stay the course and to not give up writing this book. Thank you for that. Thanks also for being the neighborhood repairman and for the good conversations while you dutifully lend your expertise to things that need repairing.

To my sister, Brenda. You generously expressed your excitement and interest when I floated the idea of writing a book about my European travel experiences that I had enjoyed a few years ago. You encouraged me to begin compiling my experiences in a book form. Thank you also for contributing to my project by providing me with a detailed version of the experience you had while reading this book.

To my parents. Thank you for teaching me the value of hard work. Also, thank you for allowing me to purchase large numbers of books with your money when I was a child. You always taught me to see the good in others; that has been a valuable asset not only throughout my travels, but also throughout the duration of my life. Thank you for all that you have done for me.

To each of my current colleagues. I only see you every few weeks. But we always have a good time when we do meet. Each of you has taught me something; thank you.

To my dog Tootsie. Thank you for teaching me patience and for always providing me with an energetic, extraordinary welcome whenever I return home, regardless how long my absence. You sure are a bundle of mischief, however, I have also learned many valuable lessons from you by simply observing your mannerisms and character. Your prolonged greetings are precious; many are the times when, upon my returns, you place your two front paws up on my knees, and stand firmly in front of me until you are done greeting me in your excited doggie way. Before we met, I had no idea that a proper "welcome back" should last for fifteen minutes!

To Edna, Elaine, Lorene, Lisa, and Kathryn. Thank you for taking good care of Tootsie whenever I leave on extended trips. It means so much to me to know that whenever I leave, she will be taken care of quite well.

Truly above all, I am grateful to God for each safe journey which He has granted me thus far. I am also thankful that I have had the opportunity to glimpse a small patchwork of His incredibly creative Creation during my journeys. Additionally, I am also considerably thankful to Him for having created such a diverse, unique network of humans which spans to the farthest ends of the earth. Each of us has been created in His image and likeness. From dust we have been created so miraculously, and to dust our bodies shall return. But our souls shall live forever.

Lastly, to anyone else who was involved in this specific book project whom I have neglected to mention; thank you.

FOREWORD

A few messages from the author's family, friends, and colleagues

Firsthand experiences of Leroy's journey to Europe is what you'll find contained within these pages and reading about the areas of where our forefathers originated was interesting to me. As always, Leroy's travels continue to give me a small peek into what the rest of the world consists of, for which I am very grateful.

Reading about the super-fast pace of the Germans while navigating through their train stations and almost getting run over by a speedy elderly lady brought a huge smile to my face. I guess I couldn't quite imagine anyone, especially an elderly lady, running over Leroy as I can recall numerous times I have walked with him in crowds, and he is usually the one out ahead and almost running over the person in front of us!

The emotions that Leroy experienced touring the Auschwitz Museum in Poland made a personal impression on me and made it all the more real for me. I have always found early 1900's history interesting and have read multiple books and articles on the Hitler era, however, seeing the photos he brought back and having Leroy describe the buildings, barbed wire fences, gas chambers, and furnaces, and everything else that he witnessed in person, made what took place in the late 1930's even more sobering. These millions of people who died at the hands of one dictator were real people with families and dreams the same as you and I have.

The excitement of launching the first book still hasn't worn off, and now the 2nd one is already being released. A special thank you to the faithful *PCBE* readers who have purchased a copy of Leroy's first book and now this one as well. Stay tuned as the way it sounds there could be some more titles coming out in the near future with all the travel plans that I keep hearing about!

I trust you will enjoy this book as much as I have, and am grateful that I crossed Leroy's path only a short 3 ½ years ago…

Raymond Lapp, publisher of PCBE

Months prior to Leroy's departure, many discussions ensued about the upcoming trip to see another land. Having never traveled abroad, it looked like quite an adventure and somewhat scary. Discussions about where to go and what to see were the foremost questions in his mind. Researching Europe, he soon decided on a few places to see. As the day drew near for him to depart, the excitement was high.

Many of us only ever had the opportunity to read about the places he was going, and to have a close friend visiting these places was exciting to all.

As the plane left the tarmac, a thousand thoughts went through his head, Leroy later admits. Having never traveled abroad the anticipation was high!

Someday I want to stay in the Ice Hotel where the beds are made of ice, and the covers are thick and plush, protecting you from the coldness of the room. Each year they carve a new house and furnishings, bringing people from all over the world! Visiting Switzerland where the finest chocolate is made is a priority for me if I ever get the opportunity to travel abroad.

Sometime in the midst of compiling this book, a new member to his family arrived. Tootsie, a Havanese-Bichon-Poodle (dog) weaved her way into his heart and they quickly have become lifelong friends. Tootsie remained a strong supporter throughout the book writing process and gives full approval to everything written! She enjoys the warm smells of the *Kamado Joe* grill while Leroy grills delicious foods. I wonder if she will be a part of his next venture when he embarks for some foreign land?

Leroy, I hope your journey can be an inspiration to everyone that has the opportunity to travel beside you as they read this book. The greatness of God's works is a wonder to all as we get a glimpse through your travels.

May you keep shining and give to God the Glory in all.

A Friend John Lapp

Follow Leroy's fast paced steps through current day Europe, traveling from Vatican City to frigid climates in Iceland. You will find that he reveals some personal feelings and experiences while traveling solo in unaccustomed cultures and languages, while still being able to make new friends and gaining a glimpse of their lifestyle and capturing culture, architecture and nature in a categorized array of photos to share with others who, like myself, have limited travel opportunities or have other obligations that keep us in close proximity to our front door.

Although I mildly disagree with Leroy that the reindeer in Finland look adorable, I appreciate his adventurous spirit, his ability to join in and gain firsthand experiences, and his passionate interest in other people's way of life, both local and abroad. He walked through the Roman Colosseum, glided through canals in Venice, rode the train through the Swiss Alps, and looked at the wooden shoes in Holland. This book is a picturesque and interesting recap on a chapter or two in social studies.

Perhaps many readers will find it of interest that their ancestry roots trace back to these lands, where you can imagine the Anabaptists enjoyed the breathtaking beauty of the mountains and villages but also suffered horribly under persecution from the State Church while holding steadfast to their faith, passing it on through generations to many of our conservative circles here in America. Within these pages are photos from actual concentration camps and some history of the grim era during World War II, when thousands of families were shattered and over a million lives savagely ended. We can take this as a fresh reminder that we have no right nor guarantee to a safe and easy life on earth, but rather to put our focus on building for eternity, and to work diligently on passing our virtues on to those following behind.

Mervin Martin

Being Leroy's oldest sister, I have watched him grow up, and knowing his love for words and of writing, this comes as no surprise that he would be writing his own books. Having read his book, *Around the World in 37 Days,* and finding his travels to Asia interesting, I have been anticipating the time when his book *European Excursions* would be printed.

Maybe due to knowing that our ancestors come from Switzerland/Germany, I enjoyed studying Europe during geography classes while in school. I have always been intrigued by the Swiss Alps. Reading of Leroy's travels there has been next best to being there and seeing the Alps myself.

I've enjoyed a few train rides in my lifetime, but riding at speeds of 180 miles an hour sounds extremely fast, and riding on a Eurostar train for 23.5 miles underneath the English Channel, hundreds of feet below sea level, would be claustrophobic for me.

Having read of the Holocaust, it was thought-provoking to see pictures of the concentration camps where so many Jews were killed. And visiting the remains of the Colosseum in Rome where many Christians are said to have perished, must have been sobering, too. Thanks to God for our time of freedom now.

The dog sled ride through Finland forests and eating in an ice restaurant would have been an experience; a somewhat chilly one, I think.

I have enjoyed reading this book.

Brenda Auker

INTRODUCTION

In December of 2017, on New Year's Eve, I boarded a plane and prepared to enjoy what would be my first extended international traveling experience. Ever curious about all that surrounds me as well as that which I cannot see, it was with eager eyes that I set out to explore Europe. Assuredly, a measurable and consistent sense of solicitude prevailed amidst all the excitement.

Within the pages of this book, I have attempted to compile a portion of the highlights of my solo journey to the European continent. Prior to this, I had never set foot in Europe, and I was quite enthusiastic to do so. I concluded that visiting the regions where early Anabaptists had lived and died would prove to be interesting. My suspicions were correct.

However, this is not a book which greatly expounds upon the history of those early Anabaptists. Rather, it is a collection of personal encounters and adventures which I had while recently traveling to the homelands of my early ancestors. While visiting many of the fascinating European cities, I tried to imagine what they might have looked like hundreds of years ago, while mired in the violent intolerance of any who defied the religious doctrines and ideologies of the State Church so many years ago.

While traveling solo on an international excursion, it is helpful to break out of one's shell, since the likelihood of meeting strangers who can quickly become friends is certainly probable. Additionally, there are also many moments in which a guarded and cautious approach towards people can be applauded, as well. Sometimes, it can be a challenge to know exactly when to peek out of that shell, and when to retreat.

Throughout my thirty-plus day journey, many valuable lessons were learned. In retrospect, it seems as if there were a multitude of moments in which I could have avoided making simple traveling errors, such as hurriedly jumping on the wrong train or absentmindedly detraining at an undesired platform or station which was not on my itinerary. Perhaps I could have avoided stumbling through darkened alleyways and sketchy regions in the middle of the night if I had done additional, extensive planning. However, if a trip is painstakingly and meticulously planned to even the most minute detail, is it even really a trip? *Probably not.* This is, of course, only my perspective. Others might take great pleasure in never experiencing a surprise, regardless how subtle, or relishing in resisting the seizure of a moment which would provide an opportunity to experience a random adventure, regardless how small.

Since I quickly passed through a few European countries and merely viewed them from the window seat of trains, you will notice that I haven't included or recorded information or experiences from all the countries which I traveled to during the winter of 2017-2018. Instead, I tried to write a few words regarding my journey in a manner of which would encapsulate the memories and arrest your attention, if only briefly.

Wherever I go, and whatever countries in which I travel to, I have discovered that the prevailing and consistent kindness of strangers is never a burden to the soul. It is this unexpected kindness that can be profoundly perplexing and extraordinarily enriching to the most transient of wayfarers. In conclusion, it is also these fleeting acts of kindness which remain seared in one's consciousness long after the visual beauty of snowcapped mountains and tranquil lakes dissipate.

— Leroy Martin

CHAPTER 1
BECOMING ACQUAINTED WITH UNFAMILIARITY

My heart began to beat a bit faster as I took an extended, final glance at all that was familiar to me. The cold December wind stung my cheeks as I stepped outside, leaving the inviting warmth behind me. I glanced at the grey, dismal skies. The makings of a snowstorm seemed to be threatening the neighborhood, nearly matching my unsettled mood.

A sense of anxiety had begun forming deep within my stomach just a few hours earlier. I glanced at my watch once more. Maybe there was still time to pull the plug on this idea of mine, which had initially taken root in my mind a few months ago.

"I'm going to call this off," I announced emphatically to a friend of mine, who I had chosen to call that afternoon, in hopes that he would encourage me to lay aside my carefully detailed plans. However, I wouldn't be that fortunate, as I quickly learned during that short phone conversation.

"You are going to do this, Leroy," my friend had remarked. "I will not allow you to back out of this. You really must go, because I know that somewhere deep down inside of you, you really do want to experience this journey, regardless of how uneasy you are right now."

And at that very moment, reality finally began to set in. It had now been officially decided. I was going to Europe, for nearly five weeks. On my own.

As I stood there in the harsh Pennsylvania winds, waiting for my driver to take me to the New Jersey airport, I had no idea of the enormous adventures which I was about to experience.

Embarking on an extensive European trip such as the one which I was attempting, is something most people would simply dream of. Perhaps this is especially true for a subset of travel-eager Anabaptists who have ancestral roots to the continent.

Some folks might rejoice at the opportunity of leaving all familiarities at home to meander amongst the archaic Roman ruins or to relish in a seemingly surreal moment as they gaze upon the majestic mountain ranges of Switzerland, their eyes feasting on the remarkable beauty that God's hand has wrought.

Still others would sigh with considerable displeasure at the thought of mingling with the masses in bustling train stations and trying to communicate effectively in a foreign language each day. To anyone who knows me, I represented a healthy dose of both these people groups. The thought of traveling to a strange, unfamiliar land where the English language isn't entirely held to standard, was somewhat unsettling—at least initially.

However, the intrigue of seeing breathtaking new lands which were filled with wonderful exploratory opportunities for solo backpackers just like myself, proved to tug quite significantly at my restless, adventurous heartstrings. The unwavering urge to explore beautiful parts of the world which my eyes had never seen before, coupled with the opportunity to immerse myself in rich, European history, proved to be measurably stronger than what my fears of the unknown were.

As a boy, I was very curious about the cultures of other people groups who lived quite differently than the people living within my home country. While attending grade school, I developed a powerful interest of traveling to other states, since the chances of me traveling to other countries at that time seemed to be untethered to reality.

Dreaming at such a young age of wonderful traveling experiences flooded my senses as I wrote handwritten letters to the tourism boards of nearly every state within the USA. In the letters, I explained that I was a grade scholar who was eager to learn more about their respective states. To my great surprise and delight, personnel working within the tourism boards of every state which I wrote to, replied in the form of a wonderful, full-color welcome packet, which contained facts, many full-color photographs, and various other information regarding their state.

Of course, this took place quite a few years ago, and I do not know if states still provide free welcome packets which contain such information. However, I do know that back then, whenever those packets arrived in my parents' mailbox, they brought a huge smile to the fresh face of a specific little boy. Had anyone told me that as an adult, I would not only be traveling throughout the United States, but to other countries as well, I really don't know how I would have responded. Perhaps with disbelief, as well as a healthy dose of excitement; I probably would have found it painful to wait until I became an adult.

Fast forwarding to the present, with the traveling dreams of a schoolboy far in the rearview mirror now, I was met with the reality of planning for my very first trip across the ocean. Prior to this trip, I had only been outside the country a few times, to neighboring countries such as Mexico, Canada, and the wee-bit-farther country of the Bahamas. My international travel experiences at this point, were very limited. Indeed, this new solo trip of mine was met with a palpable measure of trepidation and an insatiable desire to meet new people and listen to their stories, all while discovering much more of God's beautiful creation which blossoms so richly beyond my doorstep.

As I stood at the ticket counter of Newark Liberty International Airport, clutching my ticket in one hand and wrestling with my carry-on luggage in the other, little did I know that the month-long solo trip would change me and my perspectives on life in many ways that I had never conceived possible. I invite you to pack your bags (figuratively speaking) and follow me for the duration of my European adventures through the pages of this short travel book. You won't need to worry about an itinerary—I will manage all that for you.

The journey to the land of my ancestors began on the last day of 2017. My New Year's Eve was spent 40,000 feet in the air, hurtling through the atmosphere at more than five hundred miles per hour in a 787 Dreamliner. When packed in a large, steel-encased cabin filled with more than two hundred strangers high above the frigid, tumultuous waters of the mighty Atlantic Ocean, you have a tendency of hoping things will go well. At least I did.

That night, the soft lighting within the comfortable cabin of the aircraft that was produced by *Boeing*, vied to outperform the brilliant rays of the winter moon, as it cast pleasant light through the small windows of the aircraft while plying its way across the night skies.

Our New Year was welcomed high above the clouds, while traveling over the Atlantic Ocean in a cramped room filled with people hailing from many different nationalities. The night was short and rather uneventful, which is pretty much what you hope for when traveling in an airplane, and as our steel chariot pierced through the veil of thick clouds upon our descent, the people of Barcelona, Spain were already starting a new day and a brand-new year.

As the wheels of the aircraft touched down on a continent which I had never previously been to, but always wanted to visit, I began to embrace the excitement which was building with great consistency within my senses. Grabbing my backpack, I briskly made my way to the aircraft's exit point, where a staff member welcomed me to Barcelona and wished me a "lovely stay."

Passing through customs and immigration was a breeze, and the first order of the New Year was to find a taxi to transport me to my hotel room, where I wished to leave my luggage, since I wanted to explore the city in an unencumbered manner. Although it was already nearly mid-day, the city of Barcelona seemed only to be awakening. I quickly concluded that the natives here might know how to properly relax and may have discovered the secret to living an unhurried life, but a few hours later, as I was walking along the busy streets of the city, it became rather apparent that the people here seemed busy and occupied, in much the same manner as any other American city, I suppose.

Following a short drive with a taxi from my hotel which was located a few miles from the city center, I began to immerse myself in European culture. After all, if everything went well, I would spend a few weeks amongst my European pals, therefore, I might as well observe their way of life and attempt to learn something from them.

And learning is just what I did. With an observant eye, it was evident that sitting outside in comfortable chairs along the sun-soaked sidewalks of Barcelona, with a strong espresso in hand, was a respectable way to pass the time here. I decided to try it, since I felt incredibly jet lagged from my transatlantic journey. Ordering a hot beverage and a sandwich was not as simple here, it seemed, as it was in the United States, since most vendors here struggled to understand English. But I managed to get exactly what I wanted by making a few hand gestures at the menu.

I soon sat in an available chair, enjoying my espresso while soaking in the balmy breezes that found their way through the narrow, high-rise streets. Around me, chatter in a language other than English seemed to prevail, which was really my first prolonged experience of traveling to a country where my English would not always be understood well. However, after a day or two in Spain, I noticed that a measurable amount of people whom I had met within the country, could speak limited English, at least to the extent where we could roughly understand each other.

While chatting with a taxi driver, I asked him about Almeria, an area approximately six hours from Barcelona that has more plastic greenhouses erected than anywhere else on earth. Even though I wasn't a produce farmer myself, I took an interest in seeing such a sprawling area covered in plastic. The driver agreed that Almeria would indeed be a journey worth embarking upon. However, due to the lengthy duration of travel and the various travel connections I would be required to make in order to get there, I decided against traveling to the greenhouse capital of the world. Instead, I choose to read a few articles regarding the greenhouse project.

I learned that Almeria is a small area of land that sits near the basin of the Mediterranean Sea. The "Sea of Plastic," as the greenhouse project in Spain is dubbed, boasts of more than one-hundred-fifty square miles of plastic greenhouses, lined tightly side by side, and cloaks an entire area in a sea of white. The sheer amount of plastic is so vast it is said to be easily visible from space.

The vegetables grown in these massive plastic houses are generally shipped to the Scandinavian countries, such as Norway, Sweden, and Finland. The climate in these afore-mentioned countries is consistently colder when compared to other countries within Europe; and growing any vegetables successfully in Scandinavia seems to be challenging.

Following my brief conversation with the taxi driver in Barcelona, I became aware that the bulk of the labor within these greenhouses is comprised of Moroccan natives, who come to Spain to seek seasonal employment. Morocco is located within proximity to Almeria, just a relatively short distance across the Strait of Gibraltar. Most Moroccan migrant workers reportedly toil for minimum wage in Almeria, and occasionally work incredibly long hours each day at the greenhouses.

Throughout my visit to Barcelona, I basked in the summer-like breezes. The warm weather was especially a treat since back home in Pennsylvania, a cruel cold front, the results of an unusually powerful polar vortex (winter weather system), gripped the region in its icy clutches. After a quick phone call to a friend back home, it was easily confirmed that, by taking into consideration the chilly weather patterns which held my home state in its clutches, walking along the sandy beaches of Spain was considerably more relaxing and enjoyable for me than the weather patterns at home. A strong feeling of gratitude began to well up inside me; I was grateful that my friend had persuaded me to reconsider my fleeting desire of cancelling my trip to Europe at the last minute, simply because I had been a bit unsure and uncertain of traveling to Europe on my own.

Throughout the first few days of traveling within Europe, the bulk of my conversations took place with taxi drivers, as I was transported from one area of the city to the next. I later learned how to navigate the train stations, bus systems, and other methods of public transportation. Doing so effectively saved me quite a bit of money, since riding in a taxi isn't the most economical practice while traveling.

While riding along in a taxi in Barcelona, I struck up a conversation with the driver. He had been able to speak a bit of English, so I asked him where a curious tourist might go to see a bullfight, or to witness the famous *running of the bulls*. For some reason, the sight of bulls running through the streets was highly evocative whenever my thoughts turned to Spain.

I was somewhat surprised when he answered, shaking his head vigorously, and speaking with a distinct accent—which I assumed to be Spanish—that the practice had been nearly disbanded. He explained that Barcelona has outlawed the practice, while some other areas of Spain still permit such bullish games. Animal rights groups had been decrying the practice for years, he added.

Although my time in Spain had been thoroughly enjoyable, there were many other countries within the European continent that I wished to explore, so all too soon, time found me grabbing my luggage and heading for the train station to my next adventure. I quickly learned that train stations within Europe were a gateway to great adventures for all, since tourists wielding everything from surf boards and inflatable water toys to ski and snowboarding equipment, packed the expansive corridors of the stations.

Here in Europe, train stations were something to be revered, it seemed, as most times, the stations were the most elaborately constructed buildings within the cities. Again, not all stations inspired high society pomp or emitted an affluent upper-class ambiance, but large numbers of them did so in a rather consistent manner.

Before walking through the large doors of the railway station in Barcelona, I took one final glance at the city sights behind me. It had been so different from anything which I had experienced before. Small markets with vendors selling fresh fruit had been sprinkled throughout the bustling city center. Even though most elements possessed a sense of unfamiliarity, there were also a few familiarities; now that I reflect upon that day.

Going deep within my memory bank, I am able to recall an especially memorable and welcome moment of familiarity which had taken place early during my European trip while I was in Spain. The rare moment had come in the form of a welcomed sense of familiarity, as a Christmas carol—sung in English—piped melodically and wonderfully throughout the spacious halls of Barcelona's central train station. Even though most people had not spoken English well here, the holiday music which played within the railway station, as well as which emitted from the small cafes along the narrow streets, were sung primarily in English. Perhaps I wasn't as far away from home as it felt.

Many places of worship in Europe, which once held large crowds
of worshipers, have simply been reduced to museums and now
primarily serve as tourist attractions

One of the hundreds of chocolate shops which are located throughout the city of Brussels, Belgium

Watercraft docks at the mouth of the Balearic Sea

Several old churches such as this one are located throughout Ghent, Belgium

Stars line the dimly lit streets of Brussels, Belgium

A beach area which overlooks the Mediterranean Sea

A Ferris wheel, which features enclosed baskets, in Paris

Holiday decorations remained visible throughout Europe long after Christmas was past

A bustling train station, which is a typical sight throughout Europe

Barcelona is a city which features many tall, modern structures

The light of the moon softly illuminates the narrow alleys
of the city of Ghent, as trolley tracks weave their way through the streets

Barcelona caters to a host of novice seafarers

Scores of rental bikes are a common sight in Barcelona

The Sagrada Familia basilica (in Spain) is an exceptional structure,
and engineers expect to complete the final phases of construction by the year 2026

The famous Sagrada Familia basilica which has been under construction for the past 130 years

The first hotel in which the author slept during his 33-day tour of Europe

CHAPTER 2
A LESSON IN LOSSES AND EARLY BREAKFASTS

The next few days on my itinerary were eventful ones, and with great anticipation, I welcomed the idea of being whisked away to even more unfamiliar lands while nestling deep in my seat on a high-speed train which was headed for the heart of France. Considering the large amount of land which I wished to cover within a relatively short distance, it is good that I had the reliability and punctuality of Europe's high-speed trains at my disposal.

Upon my arrival at the security gates at Barcelona's train station, I fumbled around in my backpack in efforts of locating my rail pass, which would provide me ease of rail transportation throughout the duration of my time spent in Europe. Rail passes are an exceptionally affordable means of transportation here, however, foreigners are required to purchase these special *visitor* rail passes *before* arriving in Europe. The visitor rail pass which I had purchased a few weeks prior to my scheduled flight to Europe, would ensure me heavily discounted rates while traveling on the European trains.

I had paid more than one-thousand dollars for this rail pass, which would allow me to travel to twenty-six countries within Europe, with near seamless access to majority of the trains operating within those countries. So, you can imagine how distraught I became when I couldn't immediately locate my rail pass in Spain—the first country in which I was required to present the pass.

The ticket attendant didn't seem phased by my dilemma; I assumed that similar scenes of mild tragedy had unfolded in front of her eyes many times before, as flustered foreigners such as myself dug deep into their backpacks in search of their elusive rail passes. "You may take your bag over there and see if you can locate your rail pass," she said, pointing to a spot in the railway hall which was devoid of the throngs of humanity.

Walking across the occupied floors of the station, I attempted to recollect where exactly that I had placed my precious rail pass. A few minutes of frantic rummaging through my pack had proved sadly unsuccessful, as I opened every zipper of my backpack and began emptying its contents on the floor. To the unsuspecting passerby, it must surely have been a sight to behold.

A few more minutes of futile searching produced nothing, and I was sure that I had somehow lost or hastily misplaced my rail pass. There was nothing left to do but appeal to one of the ticket attendants behind the counter. Surely, they would be able to see, with a brief search on their computer, that I had indeed purchased a rail pass a few weeks ago.

As I began dejectedly repacking my belongings into my backpack, my eyes caught sight of my notebook. *I should probably make a note for myself,* I thought, *which would serve as a reminder to better secure important documents on all future trips, if I ever would decide to embark on a journey like this again.*

Reaching for my notebook was the best thing that happened to me that day, I suppose. Because as I pulled it closer, an envelope fell from the pages of the book. Hope found renewed vigor within me. Perhaps that was the envelope which I had been searching for!

It was. And with a sense of elation, I tossed the remainder of my belongings into my backpack and quickly closed the zippers. I was so excited and overjoyed at my new find, that I didn't even bother to write that personal reminder in my notepad that I had initially set out to do, just a few moments earlier. It would be an unnecessary precaution to do so, I countered, since from this point forward, I would practice greater diligence and awareness of where I placed important documents. I had learned my lesson well, I surmised; no reason to humiliate myself further with a note reminding me of this dramatic moment.

And with that, I clutched my backpack and scampered once again to the security gates, where an agent could validate my rail pass. The same agent which I had encountered approximately twenty minutes earlier, validated and stamped my ticket and wished me a safe journey.

Upon the validation of my ticket, I was required to pass through intense security, just like any other rail passenger on a select number of Europe's high-speed trains. The security procedures required me to place all my personal items and luggage on a conveyor belt, which transported the items through a large X-ray scanner. Additional security measures required any passenger to proceed slowly through a full-body scanner. No security problems were detected when I passed through, and as soon as the transportation authorities had motioned me forward, I quickly gathered my belongings and headed for my train.

While boarding my very first train on European soil, I imagine an observant person could have detected a sense of excitement on my face. I had heard stories of how fast trains travel here, and I was curious to learn if the experience would be a smooth one. Prior to this day, I had only traveled on Amtrak trains, which at times, depending on the routes, the experience was anything but smooth and relaxing.

However, now that I recall, I had also traveled briefly on a Canadian train, on an earlier journey a few years ago. That ride had been considerably smoother and more enjoyable than bouncing along the rough tracks throughout the United States.

But this upcoming train ride would be an altogether new experience. Here, on a high-speed train in Spain, headed for France, is where my journey throughout Europe was about to officially begin, I figured. Shortly after departing the city station, we passed by beautiful farmland and lush pastures.

Approximately thirty minutes after our departure at the Barcelona terminal, the operator announced that our destination in France was just a few hours away. As I settled in my seat, I marveled at the speed in which the train traveled. Objects whipped past my window at an unbelievable rate of speed. And yes, it seems my concerns regarding the smoothness of the journey had been for naught. The train ride was even better than any of the stories I had previously overheard being told by folks who had traveled to Europe and had ridden the rails here. The snow and harsh winter winds which I had left behind in Pennsylvania just a few days ago, seemed but a distant memory as I glanced out the windows of the racing train at ripe produce which was growing in the fields of Spain and France.

The rails glistened from the rays of the warm sun and appeared to follow the train cars, remaining perfectly aligned and within harmony of our moving rail cars. Sometime throughout the journey, I cast my eyes across the horizon and observed a few horses which were being trained by their owners on a nearby horse ranch. Spanish bungalows littered the countryside as we continued to pass by at a rapid pace.

A few hours into the journey, I witnessed several dozen bright pink flamingos that were perusing around the swampy waters, a short distance from the tracks. The train operator continued to deftly navigate the slight turns along the tracks with such ease, and for a moment, I wondered what it might be like to be the operator of a high-speed train which transported hundreds of humans to their desired destinations.

Throughout my musings, we left the flamingos deep in the distance, and zipped past countless acres of vineyards. Vineyards were sprawled densely across the countryside and seemed to be a dime a dozen here in France. The country produces between seven and eight billion bottles of fine wine annually. From all the countries in the world, France is one of the world's largest producers of wine.

The people whom I met in France seemed abundantly friendly, even though the language barrier was significant here as well. Most people, when asked if they could speak English, smiled and replied, "Not very well."

The French folks wore a ready smile wherever they went, it seemed, much to the contrast of a statement a young Frenchman had made to me. "No one smiles here in the city," he had declared. But to me, a wandering American tourist, the French appeared more approachable and amiable when compared to the reserved and indifferent faces of Americans within large cities, such as Manhattan. Perhaps we perceive people of our own nationality differently.

Throughout my time in France, meeting with locals at a coffee shop or a quaint café, and opening lines of dialogue became a challenge, albeit a rewarding one. By attempting to speak with foreigners in (sometimes) choppy conversation, I learned that while the language barriers are, on occasion, really frustrating, we humans, regardless what language we speak or which country we call home, often have more commonalities in place than not. For example, even though I couldn't speak their native language very well, the French people seemed impressed and grateful that I would take an interest in their lives.

While passing through Paris for the first time in my life, my eyes could scarcely seem to behold everything which was taking place. Hundreds of cars whipped past pedestrian-laden sidewalks as each human being tried to get from point A to B in the least amount of time possible.

It was interesting to set wondering eyes upon the majestic monuments which were erected so prolifically throughout this affluent French city. Most of the stone, granite, and marble monuments appeared to have been built hundreds of years ago. Even the poetic French architecture appeared somewhat engaging and seemed to have developed its own character. After stopping to read a few plaques which were written in several languages, including English, and were located at some of the beautifully constructed buildings, I learned that a good portion of the buildings had been completed a few hundred years ago.

While driving through the city immediately upon my arrival via train, my taxi driver must have noticed that I was staring at the immensely complex structures with disbelieving eyes. In spite of my astonishment, he smiled and said something which surprised me, "Yes, Paris is a small town, not a big city." I looked at him as though he were making a joke. Here I had been thinking the exact opposite and was admiring the intricate details of the large monuments and elaborately designed architecture which had been built so many years ago.

Trying to save face, I explained to him that it is my first visit to Paris, to which he quickly extended a hearty welcome to me. He then became insistent, as he encouraged me to stay for several days, however, I hadn't planned to stay that long in Paris, so I explained to him that I am on a tight schedule, and perhaps I could return some other time. My response seemed satisfactory to him, and he seemed to relax.

The following morning I was awakened by the sound of rain lashing against the small windows of my third story hotel. It wasn't quite daylight yet, and the streetlights of Paris twinkled below as pedestrians and motorists maneuvered through the heavy raindrops.

Nearly an hour later, I walked around the still sleepy city, searching for an establishment that would be not be averse to serving breakfast at such an early hour. The search continued for some time, but eventually, my food-hunting efforts were fruitful. I noticed a waiter placing a large boarded breakfast menu outside along the sidewalk, and eagerly seeking refuge from the cruel pelting of the lashing rain, I inquired if I could stop in for a bite to eat. The waiter looked at his watch, and acknowledged that it is still early, but agreed to serve me.

I took advantage of the moment and was grateful for the respite of the persistent raindrops which the establishment provided. The ambiance of the upscale diner was rather subdued due to the early hour, but I didn't mind at all as I enjoyed a hearty breakfast of scrambled eggs and bacon.

The waiter was very friendly and lingered for conversation even as locals began trickling in steadily. Very intrigued that someone such as myself would be undertaking a month-long, solo trip abroad, the young Frenchman had dozens of questions for me. He spoke English very well, and at this point in the trip I was missing conversation considerably, so this was one of the rare moments in which I cherished such early morning dialogue.

"You woke up too early, if you really are on vacation, you need to stay in bed till at least nine o'clock," he explained heartily. "You are no longer in America; it is time for you to slow down."

We continued our lively dialogue, as I, too, asked him a bunch of questions about his country. It is really fascinating to talk with people of a different background, culture, and religion. I am inclined to believe that we can learn something from everybody whom we meet in life, and I had a mindset to do just that on my journey throughout Europe.

Applauding me for my adventurous traveling spirit, the waiter at the restaurant went on to explain that he had waited on the tables of many Americans, but that there is something different about me, even though I, too, am American. He continued to explain that most Americans which he had served at the restaurant, were intolerant to other cultures and indifferent to their practices. "I can tell that you are generally interested in our culture, and that is good," he had said, smiling approvingly.

Of course, I couldn't have gone to France without penciling a visit to the Eiffel Tower into my itinerary. The tower is probably the country's most famous landmark. One morning, I walked for more than an hour along the sidewalks of the city, using my GPS to guide me to the heavily visited spot where hundreds of other folks had already beat me to.

The queue was intimidating, and it would have taken approximately three hours until I was able to get into the building. So, I quickly snapped a few photos and went to see a few other less famous—and therefore less crowded—landmarks within the city.

Paris had a population of more than 2.24 million residents when I visited, and it seems as though winter doesn't agree with them well. Men and women were bundled up in scarfs and heavy gloves, and the temperature was in the mid-50s. Some people were even sporting earmuffs. A few of the folks complained that it is unfortunate that I am visiting their beautiful city when it is so cold and blustery. The wind held steady at twelve miles per hour, no gale-force winds to contend with, and in my opinion, the temperature was quite balmy compared to where I had just traveled from. Therefore, I had thought that it had been an excellent time to visit Paris.

Everything in Europe is different, and it took quite a bit of time until I had become adequately adjusted. The train timetables are displayed in twenty-four-hour readouts instead of the typical twelve-hour systems which are primarily used within the United States. Most of Europe does not use the Imperial system. You can imagine that it was rather interesting the first few times within my hotel rooms, until I had managed to find the ambient temperature while using the Celsius as a measure of temperature instead of the far more acquainted Fahrenheit system. After tweaking the thermostat for what seemed like a dozen times, I finally found the *Goldilocks zone*—a temperature which seemed just right for me.

As I began preparing to leave the city, I assumed that it is through the lens of which we observe different cultures which make them appear so endearing and charming. As a visitor from America, I had found the city of Paris to be warm and inviting, while the locals had warned me that many of its people are aloof and indifferent.

A few nights after I had arrived, I sat under the soft moonlight along a small side street corner within the city, enjoying a refreshing gelato before I departed for yet another country.

If you ever have the opportunity of visiting the charming little city of Brussels, Belgium, you probably shouldn't decline. The city, which is surrounded by Germany and The Netherlands, serves as the powerful political seat of Europe, in much the same way as Washington DC is the seat of political power within the United States.

There is much more to see here in Brussels besides politically charged activities, however, and I especially found it pleasant to take a leisurely stroll down to the Grand Place, which is the city's well-known, beloved square. I visited during the Christmas season; therefore, many decorations and lights had been strung, cloaking the square in a shimmering light show. Of all the memorable experiences which I enjoyed throughout this trip, the evening which I spent walking through (and spending some time in) the Grand Place will remained etched in my memory for quite some time.

I had chosen to explore the city shortly upon my arrival late one night in early January. It was a very cold night, one which nearly convinces you to remain indoors while basking in the warmth of a crackling fireplace in a hotel lobby. But instead, I braved the winter winds and was surprised at how easy it was to enjoy the cheerful ambiance of the quiet little city that night.

Brussel's captivating architecture came to life as I hurried along the nearly deserted, windswept streets, pulling my winter cap over my ears a bit more to fully utilize the comforting fabric to my advantage. The square was nearly abandoned due to the late hour, and it felt as if I were exploring the city all by myself. There were, however, two police vans loaded with armed officers who, I assume, stood guard throughout the duration of the night, where the Grand Place was located.

Soft echoes drifted on the winter breezes whenever a few random folks would enter the square. Gasping at the towering steeple which sat prominently atop the attractive buildings within the square, I decided that it might be interesting to find a semi-comfortable place to sit and observe the small crowds of people that seemed to gather here at the square. Perhaps most of them were also tourists, since there was a whole lot of photographs being taken by them.

I continued to sit in silence for a moment while contemplating how humans would even go about constructing such a complicated architectural masterpiece. During the few years which I worked within the commercial construction industry,

I was aware that fancy buildings like these are certainly complicated and time-consuming to design and construct. The night continued to march along slowly, and an increasing chill became ever persistent, persuading me to return to my warm hotel room. Clutching my winter jacket a bit tighter, I reluctantly chose to end the day's adventures and slowly began ambling through the dimly lit, cobblestone streets toward my hotel room.

On my way back that night, I took notice of the many fine chocolate shops which seemed to occupy every available space along the streets of Brussels. Even though I don't much care for the taste of chocolate, I realized that I should probably have my passport revoked if I didn't indulge in some Belgian chocolates during my stay. Upon making a late-night purchase at one of the open shops, I carefully savored some of the finest chocolate which Belgian had to offer. There was no bitter aftertaste associated with the candy, therefore, I concluded that there are indeed worse things to eat than chocolate.

Fancy arches are abundant throughout many countries and cities in Europe

Belgium's Grand Place evokes a sense of grandeur and pomp

Reflections of the tower appear in a puddle of muddied water in Paris

The blurred image of a mother and children walking past the stately structures in Belgium

The Arc de Triomphe along France's Champs-Elysees

The Eiffel Tower pierces the skyline of Paris

The Eiffel Tower, which was built in record time, was completed in March of 1889

The entrance to the Louvre, in Paris, France, is one of the most famous museums in the world

Visions of nightlife at the Grand Place in Belgium

Two police officers stand close to their vehicle while maintaining a close watch on the nighttime visitors to the Grand Place

CHAPTER 3
GERMAN CONFUSION AND ITALIAN PERFECTION

While in Germany, I was introduced to a crash course in European train travel. No, there were no crashes which occurred throughout my travels; however, I was required to learn an entirely new method of traveling—seemingly on the spot.

As my itinerary would have it, Germany was the third country which I visited. Here, it was proven that I was still a novice at riding the rails. In my opinion, the country's expansive rail system is unbelievably frenetic and cruelly chaotic. Observing thousands of German folks milling and rushing about on the numerous platforms is enough to leave any American traveler a bit disoriented.

In the United States, nearly everyone who goes on a day trip with me complains that they can't keep up when we are walking, and that they want me to slow my step, since they believe I simply walk too fast for them.

But it was different here. In Germany, I was the one who walked too slow, and seemed to nearly get trampled underfoot of several fast-walking German folks. I started to question if I was way out of my element.

Here, deep within Europe, I was utterly lost and perplexed as to how the massive, complex train systems operated. In my defense, it probably didn't help that the train schedules were announced and printed in the German language. This was difficult for me to comprehend, since I had pretty much failed every German class I took while in grade school.

I also felt somewhat overwhelmed by the swarming net of humanity that seemed to close in on me at every turn as I slowly walked the corridors of the train stations, while wearing a startled, perplexed look on my American face.

Men in tailored business suits with briefcases slung over their shoulders, millennials with backpacks and trendy carry-ons, mothers with strollers, even sweet grandmas and grandpas were efficiently shuffling about, vying for the premium seats during the initial seconds in which the trains arrived at their platforms. Except me—

everything seemed to move a bit too fast for me. I guess I hadn't been in Europe quite long enough at this point. In time, I became much better at jumping onto trains at a moment's notice, seconds before they depart.

While I paused to look up at the schedule board, I dodged at the last minute to narrowly avoid being run into by a speedy elderly lady. She seemed to be moving too fast for her age, but then again, I too, needed to pick up my pace by the looks of things.

Narrowly avoiding that human collision, by this time I was both humiliated and breaking into a mild sweat. In efforts to retain some form of dignity, I will refrain from sharing with you the exact number of times that I exited my train at the wrong station in Germany, since the departure had been announced in a language that was foreign to me. Neither will I disclose how often I jumped aboard the wrong train. It really was not my most favorite country to visit.

But I can tell you that I regained my composure around noon on the third day of my train travels throughout Europe. It is rather disheartening that it took so long for me to gain a foothold and retain my good senses, but I will tell you, it was all part of a solid learning experience. After my initial struggles with boarding the correct trains at the correct times on the correct platforms, I was rather buoyant each time that I managed to arrive at the desired platforms and board the desired trains from here on.

A few train stations throughout Europe consisted of over thirty different tracks and platforms. The central train station in Zurich, a major travel hub within the country of Switzerland, boasted over forty platforms. Within these expansive, central train stations, sometimes there were as many as a dozen departures, all staggered within mere minutes of each other on a host of platforms.

Majority of railway stations throughout Europe have more than one level of platforms, some even have five or six levels, each containing a complicated labyrinth of tracks and platforms. Bearing this in mind, it is within an inexperienced traveler's best interests to arrive on the correct level, at the correct platform in plenty of time; better to wait a while than to rush around frantically, running from one level to the next, minutes before your departure. (Yes, I did this a few times).

Ninety percent of Europe's mass transit rail system is operated on electricity. Only a few touristy trains which specialize in traveling to exotic locations are powered by diesel, but even those trains are quickly moving towards being replaced or upgraded to electric operating systems.

The train systems in Europe are considerably dependable and cannot be compared to the American rail systems which I am all too familiar with. For example, the wait time generally never exceeded twenty-five minutes while I was waiting on a connecting train in Europe. With such an impressive, ultra-reliable rail system, it is quite possible to visit two (or more) countries within the same day.

However, when attempting to travel to more than one country within a day, a traveler might be required to purchase several tickets and board perhaps two or three connecting trains when visiting different countries or cities within a one-day time frame. This isn't such a problem, really, and the overall convenience of it is, that a traveler will generally not be required to wait two or three hours between each of those (station) connections.

Realistically, from my experience while traveling throughout Europe during early winter, the extent of the waiting time will most likely gravitate towards twenty minutes. This may not be true during the summer months when tourism peaks and the passenger trains quickly fill to capacity, or in the event that a winter storm bears down on the region. However, all things considered, a twenty-minute wait time is probably a good rule of thumb, as they say.

During the slower winter season, when throngs of tourists were flocking in droves towards warm, sunny beaches instead of to colder regions within Europe, I consistently had the pleasure of traveling on any train, on which I wished to be a passenger. Easy, unfettered access to the train of my choice was certainly appreciated, and left me feeling spoiled, as if I didn't quite deserve such ease of transportation across the continent. (This feeling, of course, took place after I had become more comfortable mastering the train systems here).

In Germany, a train is referred to as a *zug* and a seat as *sitzplatz*. While in Italy, trains are referred to as *treno* and tickets are called *billiettes*.

Bahnhof means railway in Switzerland, and in the Czech Republic, platform is spelled *peron* and track is referred to as *tor*. In the Netherlands, a platform is called a *spoor* and a train a *trein*. As you can imagine, there is a considerable learning curve when traveling abroad, but each time that you manage to succeed in your attempts to travel from one country to the next, you become increasingly confident. There really isn't much that matches the excitement of looking at your freshly printed station tickets and knowing the trains will take you pretty much where you want to go faster than you thought you needed to get there.

On one particular night while I was visiting Germany, the rain fell hard, and the wind gusts blustered mercilessly. Throughout my travels, I quickly understood that there is one thing that happens regularly in Europe during the winter months; and that is dismal, gloomy weather.

As the storm raged outside, I glanced out the windows of the train and snuggled deeper under the thin blanket which the train attendant had provided for me, as was customary on an overnight train. I was grateful for the warmth and safety which the dry, heated rail car offered as it hummed along rhythmically on the tracks in the middle of the night.

The sound of the heavy downpour unleashing buckets of cold precipitation on the roof and sides of the window was comforting, to an extent. Attempting to peer through the darkness outside was rather futile. The heavy rain required passengers to wield their umbrellas as they dashed through the puddles of water whenever we arrived at a station stop.

While traveling to Italy via the Austrian-owned and operated *NightJet* railcar, I met many people. A couple, who was highly conversational, shared that they were from Norway and were traveling for several days. The man and woman talked with me for several hours. They were generous and shared some food with me as well as a host of interesting tips regarding traveling within Europe. When they learned that I was on my way to Italy, they began telling stories of how they visited the country not so long ago.

Having been from Norway, they also possessed a vast scope of knowledge about the colder countries within Europe. They surmised that Finnish people are perhaps the strangest people in Europe. This people group excels at strange outdoor activities and holds an annual outdoor music festival each year in bitterly cold temperatures, the couple told me. They also added that majority of the people in Europe readily consider Finnish behavior to be unique. Well, their stories were fascinating, but didn't deter me from desiring to visit Finland, since that country had been on my itinerary before I even left America.

As I indicated previously, communicating in Germany was a significant hurdle for me to overcome, and from the host of countries which I visited on this journey, less people spoke basic English in Germany than within the rest of the countries combined.

Even so, in Germany I confided to one person whom I met who spoke English fluently, and I expressed my desire to become better familiarized with the German language and the many dialects which are spoken there. "I wish that I could learn the German language within an hour, so that I could communicate more effectively," I had said to him.

He laughed, and replied in English, "Don't you worry, son, life is too short to learn German. You are doing just fine if you know English." Somehow, I suppose I felt a little better knowing that.

Language is a fascinating thing, for sure. And I imagine that if God hadn't scrambled the one language that was spoken by humans during the construction of the Tower of Babel, we humans throughout the world may very well still speak the same language. Out of one, God certainly made many.

It is estimated that slightly more than 1.5 billion people in the world can speak English very well, while out of this same number, more than four hundred million speak English as their second language. In 2015, sixty-seven countries out of one-hundred-ninety-five, relied on English as their primary language, but this does not entirely mean that it is the first language that all the residents of these countries speak. They simply *know* how to speak the English language.

Additionally, I believe the French language is the most beautiful and eloquent of all the languages which have reached my ears so far, since it appears to flow so fluidly, akin to that of a rippling stream.

While the United Nations recognizes more than two-hundred nations and territories on earth, the United States only recognizes that there are *less* than two-hundred countries (195). For example, there are quite a few self-declared countries that fail to have gained recognition by some or any UN members, but they still operate in an independent manner from the countries which claim them.

The constant, melodic humming of the rails had lulled me to sleep the previous night. If you are inclined to assume that spending a night in a moving train which is heading through the snow-covered Austrian mountains under the soft light of a winter moon sounds delightful, you are not entirely mistaken.

However, you should realize that the quality of sleep that you'll be subjected to within a moving rail car is certainly not as satisfying of a sleep as you would expect to receive while lying in a soft bed within a stationary room in your home. Nevertheless, the experience was still an appealing one. The gentle, consistent rocking of a rail car might be a great idea to soothe a crying baby to sleep, but most adults whom I have spoken to aren't as keen to motion while they are trying to catch a night of rest.

Early that morning, I was stirred by the train attendant calling out my name in a rather urgent manner. I assumed that he had been calling my name previously a few times, perhaps. I had a private room, so I quickly jumped out of bed and opened the door a bit, to determine what the fuss was all about.

The attendant stood there, and addressing me in high German, he said in a most cheerful manner, "Guden Morgen, Mr. Leroy."

In his hands was a platter of delicious breakfast morsels. These were for me, he indicated. Continuing, the attendant explained simply, "Fruhstuck." To which I replied, "What?"

As he nudged the platter closer to me, it became increasingly apparent that he indeed intended me to accept the food. Still groggy from the unsettled night of sleep which I endured while on the train, I made every effort to graciously accept the meal which the attendant had brought to me.

The luxurious accommodations of purchasing a night ticket included a simple breakfast platter served on a warm white plate. It was comforting to know that even though the Germans were difficult to understand when they spoke, they still placed priority on the service with which they provided me, their American guest. As I munched on the heated turkey sandwich and consumed the hot beverage, I realized that I could quickly get used to such great service.

Moments after I had consumed the last morsels of my breakfast, my lengthy train ride which I was on was finally reaching its conclusion. The persistent rain had subsided, leaving everything a cold and slippery mess. I disembarked the train when we arrived at the station in Italy, and carefully made my way through the pre-dawn darkness along the narrow, brick-paved streets of Florence, Italy. There, within the city, approximately a twenty-minute walk from the train station, I found a locker at a hotel where I left my luggage while I went on my way exploring the city. That morning, as the Italian dawn began to break in earnest, I observed a great deal of bicyclists as they headed towards their place of employment.

That day, I was kept busy walking throughout the city, while I spent a great deal of time visiting the largest basilica in Florence. Upon the conclusion of my self-guided tour, and after my curiosities had been settled, I decided it would be best to hop aboard another high-speed Italian train, which would carry me away in near-lightning speed, to the historic city of Rome.

The Vatican City, the seat of global Catholic power, is located within Rome, and is one of the smallest countries, per capita. The City is recognized by the United Nations as a separate, sovereign country, and the Vatican does not abide by all the laws which other countries might. In another chapter, I will share some of the experiences which I had while I toured this unique country/city. First, let's explore the ruins of ancient Rome just a bit.

A high fence discourages tourists from strolling too closely through the ancient ruins of the Roman Forum

A portion of the Cathedral of Santa Maria del Fiore is flooded with tourists. Construction for the cathedral reportedly began in the late 13th century.

An expansive government building in Berlin, Germany

Brandenburg Gate, Berlin's most recognized and famous landmark.

Guards, sporting brightly colored attire, stand watch at the entrance to the Vatican

Intimidating columns weave elegantly along Saint Peter's Square

Many ancient buildings can be seen while strolling through the now-modern streets of Rome

Massive columns span the majestic structures within Vatican City

Santa Maria Novella, an ornately designed worship building in Florence, Italy

Saint Peter's square in Vatican City

The dome of Saint Peter's Basilica is seen from a distance

The iconic monument (Brandenburg Gate) in Berlin, Germany was constructed between 1788 and 1791

CHAPTER 4
ANCIENT RUINS AND GLIDING GONDOLAS

The day was already half spent by the time I arrived in the city of Rome. I had traveled to Italy from Belgium and enjoyed the lengthy train ride. There had been a few connections throughout the journey, which required me to disembark a few times, and board connecting trains which then transported me to sunny Italy. I was eager to leave the dreary skies and chilly weather of Belgium behind me.

I would like to take a few moments to discuss some of the food differences between several of the European countries which I visited, before we take an extensive tour of the ancient ruins which remain in now modern Rome.

Without a doubt, Italians have known their way around dough for quite some time, and the pizza and pastas they carefully, masterfully created for me, tasted rather wonderful. The Italian desserts which were prevalently offered in restaurants were tempting and dangerously laden with sugar.

Certainly, there is something strangely relaxing about eating authentic Italian pizza while floating lazily down a canal and having the gondolier earn his wages by rowing the gondola while your senses take in all the sights and smells of Venetian culture.

The French also do a lot of things well, and they may even be the self-described perfectionists when it comes to pastries, but that is of course, up for discussion. However, there may be nothing more delightful in Europe than the wonderful taste of French pastries, and I am not even that much of a dessert guy. The mouth-watering pastries did look delicious though, and often, I found them difficult to resist. Additionally, the French folks also took breakfast seriously, and the scrambled eggs that were served in restaurants were unusually fluffy and light.

Upon discussing the pursuit of perfection of the French, I would likely be remiss if I failed to address that such ideology and ambition is also seemingly prevalent among the Italian folks. Throughout my travels, it appeared that the energetic Italians tried to outperform all other Europeans.

In Italy, the bulk of taxi drivers operated *Teslas,* an expensive and premium electric motor vehicle. It appeared as if having a nice car was of great importance here. By casual observance, it also seemed probable to conclude that Italians are always in a considerable hurry to get somewhere—much like the Germans, I guess.

For example, Italy has high-speed trains capable of reaching exhilarating speeds of up to two-hundred miles per hour. Some of the fastest trains in Europe are found in Italy—if I am not mistaken.

Upon arriving in the Italian city of Florence, which is world-famous for designing exquisite leathers for the wealthy, I strolled through a few touristy shops, and was quite surprised at the sheer number of leather shops which lined the streets. There must have been more than three-hundred vendors selling their fine leather goods.

The weather couldn't have been more perfect when I paid Italy a little visit during January 2018. Walking through the Roman ruins of the Colosseum was quite memorable, to say the least. A sense of excitement was present within me as I stood near the arena where fierce Roman gladiators had waged their battles, hundreds of years ago. Entertaining large crowds was something which the Romans excelled at, and judging by their exquisite architecture and monuments, they certainly possessed a flair for the arts and high drama.

As I meandered about the expansive Colosseum, my mind was filled with many thoughts. The moment provided an occasion for reflection upon the history of this once great and powerful nation (Rome).

It was both sobering and exciting to imagine what the ancient gladiators must have felt while they stood and fought against their opponents. What thoughts might have taken place within their minds prior to the gladiator games? Did human emotions such as fear find its way into their hearts? Surely, some of them knew they faced certain death while being pitted in a savage fight to the death against a mightier opponent. Perhaps some of them shut their hearts and minds to the fear which threatened to gnaw at their insides.

According to several historical documents, the ancient Colosseum measured 620 x 513 feet. It is also believed that the mighty concrete structure was built within ten years, a significant feat for that era. The Colosseum which I saw in Rome, is said to have been one of the first free-standing structures of such magnitude which was built from concrete and stone. The previous amphitheaters which had been constructed by the Romans were partially built into hillsides, in efforts of adding support to the large structures.

Still standing (partially) today, the distinctive Colosseum consists of three stories—of which some portions have since fallen into disrepair. The entrances were arched majestically and are said to have provided a sense of grandeur to all who entered.

A total of approximately eighty entrances such as the ones previously described, were supported by semi-circular columns. The design was certainly lavish at that time—even for Rome—and adequately portrayed the decadence which became the epitome of the Roman Empire. To the rest of the civilized world, Rome was a symbol of great power, wealth, and high society. On the outside, Rome may have looked educated and suave, however, as history tells us, on the inside, the country was all too prone to vices and indulgences, and possessed an extremely cruel and harsh personality, especially to those who disagreed with the Roman rule.

This notoriously well-known Colosseum was also the site where many believe that scores of Christians took their final breath on this earth. A collection of historical books have been written that depict the heinous deaths of Christians within the grand arena of the Colosseum. *However, a disturbingly vast number of articles (from prominent universities) and information placards (throughout Rome, 2018) regarding the history of the notorious Colosseum, claim that while Christians died here, they were not specifically killed for their faith, but merely slaughtered as an overall part of the normal events (blood sports) which took place here.*

It is not unusual, I guess, that current Rome would wish to distance itself from a history of horrible Christian persecutions which still many historians conclude took place throughout a dark period of time here. Additionally, several religious scholars agree that St. Ignatius was the first Christian to have been persecuted publicly, in front of a cheering crowd consisting of tens of thousands of people, in ancient Rome.

Sometime during A.D. 80, shortly upon the opening of the Colosseum, the sprawling amphitheater reportedly hosted one-hundred days of games. Some of these games consisted of gladiatorial combats as well as wild animal fights.

It is believed that on more than one special occasion, the arena floor of one of the several large entertainment venues here was flooded with water and spectacular naval games—which is said to have involved gruesome deaths—took place. Majority of the participants in these special mock naval exercises were prisoners which are believed had been already sentenced to death for their crimes.

Historians conclude that the beautifully constructed Colosseum was used for deadly games and other heathen events for the duration of no less than four centuries.

It was interesting for me to observe the structures which these ancient civilizations had erected, so many hundreds of years ago. By all appearances, they indeed knew how to build majestic, intimidating buildings.

The sun was beating down in a merciless manner, encouraging me to search for the perfect spot that might serve as a welcome respite from the intense rays of the Italian sun. Although it was a clear day in January, the sun seemingly managed to unleash its heat and energy quite well. Seeking the welcome shade of umbrella pine trees, I sat down in the grass and enjoyed a solo picnic. With the impressive Roman ruins (ancient buildings) serving as a breathtaking backdrop, I surmised that this was probably as good as my trip was going to get. *I am happy to inform you that I was very incorrect.*

It was a wonderful spot, this secluded area which I had found, and I nestled between several lofty trees, indulging in a few moments of solitude and self-reflection. This was also, perhaps, a wonderful place where a writer might easily gather inspiration for future projects.

Today, there seems to be no end to money within the city of Rome, and the police officers here drove luxurious *Range Rovers*—the expensive SUVs which are sought after by the wealthy.

I also saw more *Smart* cars in one day while visiting Rome than I collectively saw during my entire life within the United States. Another observation of mine concluded that European drivers also park so closely to each other that they can barely open their doors to get out of their cars. This behavior simply didn't seem to make sense to me. I am sure that parking spots are coveted within the city, however, I couldn't help but think that this type of parking behavior would certainly not be acceptable in America.

For the duration of the first full week of my European travels, I had slept in a different country each night and was exposed to a different language each day. This proved to be extremely exhausting, but I was traveling at my own pace, so if I wanted things to slow down, I knew exactly with whom I needed to consult.

An elderly gentleman whom I had met during my time in sun-soaked Italy, engaged me in some weather conversation when he learned that I was from the United States. He explained that he had heard that regions within the United States were experiencing an exceptionally harsh winter pattern, and he mentioned that he would enjoy it if I taught him how to properly pronounce the word *freezing*.

Well, I expected that a light task in linguistics such as this was going to be rather easy. But it wasn't. After nearly eight attempts at saying the simple word, the Italian gentleman finally got it right. I was somewhat amused. With a big grin on his face, he repeated the word successfully a few more times before heartily thanking me for teaching him a previously unfamiliar English word. I guess a few rather unique friendships were formed throughout my journey to Europe.

Then there was also the Italian taxi driver that didn't wish to accept my credit card as a reputable method of payment. I had been completely out of European currency and hadn't taken the time to hit the ATM prior to jumping in his car. I sheepishly informed him that I didn't have any Euros, and upon hearing this, he seemed considerably displeased. His face clouded with a look which I assumed was a mixture of extreme indigestion and repulse.

Before I could even suggest it, he inquired if I have any American cash on me. I responded that I do. This seemed to cheer him up again, and he graciously accepted the twenty dollars which I had. Placing the money on the seat beside him, before the car even came to a halt, I watched with delight as his frown completely disappeared. He smiled widely. It seems like money—at least in his situation— can buy happiness after all; of course, the fleeting kind.

After I exited the taxi car, I eagerly made my way to historical Vatican City. I had been looking forward to visiting this small country—actually, the smallest country in the world.

The city/country consists of less than one-hundred-twenty-five acres. The small sovereign state had a population of less than nine-hundred people in 2019. The primary residents living within the City are priests and nuns, comprised of diverse nationalities from many corners of the world. Vatican City is surrounded by the historical Italian city of Rome. The City has been affectionately dubbed as the *Holy See.*

The smallest independent country in the world also has its own post office, police force, hospital, and its own bank. (The Euro, a type of paper currency used throughout many countries in Europe, can be spent here, and is often the preferred method of payment when purchasing items with cash).

Bankers throughout the world have estimated that the Vatican City (which is not the same as the Vatican Church) has an estimated financial worth between ten and fifteen billion dollars. However, no one outside the Vatican seems to know with definitive proof exactly how much the Vatican (country) is worth. The country is said to have made considerable investments within the steel, chemical, insurance, real estate, and construction industries.

Major languages which are spoken within the City are Latin and Italian. Powerful transmitters which are located throughout the city have the capacity for reaching massive audiences, as they listen to the special radio broadcasts which the Pope conducts, on occasion. The City is also home to the Pope, who is the highest human religious authority figure within Catholicism.

A 2016 *Pew Research* study found that more than eighty percent of Italian residents are somehow affiliated with the Catholic Church. According to figures which were compiled by the *World Christian Database* in 2010, Italy had the highest concentration of Catholics than any other country throughout Europe. Numbers gathered by *WCD* throughout the same year, concluded that the highest number of people practicing the Catholic faith throughout the African continent are located within the DR Congo. Additionally, per figures provided by the Vatican, there are an estimated total of 1.2 billion Roman Catholics throughout the world.

One must only travel to Europe in order to gain perspective of exactly how prevalent Catholicism is within Europe—there were reminders of the Church spread prolifically throughout the nineteen countries which I visited.

In many countries throughout the world, Catholics have their own schools. As of 2011, the Catholic Church operated the largest non-governmental school system in the world. Throughout the years, there have been reportedly more than ten Catholic justices appointed to the *United States Supreme Court.*

Even with the large numbers of practicing Catholics spread throughout Europe, many surveys indicate that the numbers of practicing Christians have been in steep decline here in Europe within the past thirty years.

At this particular point of the journey, however, I need to hurry along if I wish to catch my train which is headed for the water-logged city of Venice. Upon my arrival, I hope to enjoy a relaxing ride on a gondola, as it gleefully glides on the gentle waters of the various canals which slice through the picturesque Italian city of Venice.

Ancient gladiators fought to the death within the Colosseum. Many early Christians also perished here, most times in gruesome, merciless fashion

Ancient ruins in proximity of the Roman Forum, Italy

Buildings appear in ruin at the Roman Forum on Palatine Hill, Italy

Statues adorn nearly every important structure throughout Rome

Commissioned between 70-80 AD, the Colosseum was the pride of ancient Rome

Eight sturdy columns are what remains of the Temple of Saturn, built by the Romans.
It is widely believed that the temple was dedicated in 497-498 BC.

More ruins at the Roman Forum

Small pieces of stone, that once represented buildings and monuments, now lie at the Roman Forum

The Arch of Constantine, near the Roman Colosseum, was constructed in 312 AD to honor emperor Constantine the Great

The great Roman Colosseum, the site of many gruesome, unspeakable activities,
was the entertainment center for the ancient Romans

Trees grow abundantly in proximity of the Colosseum, which was built by ancient Rome

The majestic remains of the Colosseum in Rome

Whispers of a once great and fearsome global superpower remain in modern Rome

The columns remain of an ancient Roman temple in the Forum. The columns are referred to as The Three Sisters

CHAPTER 5
TINY ELEVATORS AND BIG HOSPITALITY

Canals and gondolas are ubiquitous within the tiny Italian city of Venice, as some of you may already know. As a scholar, I looked, with eager eyes, at photos of gondolas gliding along the city's canals, with the gondoliers standing upright, deftly navigating their watercraft. I had wondered what it would be like to receive a ride on such a unique boat.

A few minutes after I stepped off the platform at the Santa Lucia train station in Venice, it seemed as if I had traveled to another planet, perhaps. The modern train station was built right along one of the largest canals, and the impressive canal is one of the first things which a passenger sees upon disembarkation. There are many unique train stations throughout Europe, but the Santa Lucia station is probably one of the most memorable to me, in terms of its immediate proximity to such a large canal.

I had arrived within the city late on a Saturday night, and throngs of tourists were bustling about the streets. It was difficult to maneuver the crowded streets with my luggage, and I was glad that I didn't need to walk far until I reached my hotel. Upon checking into my room, I took a short nap before I went outside to wrestle with the masses again.

By the time I had exited the hotel, dusk had fallen, and a steady rain was drenching the area. A bit disheartened, I purchased a cheap umbrella and trudged through the crowds of people who were apparently not dissuaded from their planned activities of the evening. After buying a few souvenirs, I found a nice pizza shop where I enjoyed authentic Italian pizza once again. (I am afraid that this became a bit of a habit of mine while in Europe).

The following day, the sun shone brightly, and I explored the canal-rich city once again, this time leaving my umbrella behind. A large canal slices through the center of the city, and a stately foot bridge serves as a source of connection between either side of the city. Numerous alleyways snake through the city, and bicycles and boats seemed to be the primary source of transportation here, unless, of course, you chose to walk.

Early that morning, along one of these alleyways I met a gondolier who was maintaining his craft. As I walked by, he asked if I would like a ride. He must have seen the inquisitive way in which I had looked upon the strange-looking boat. I replied that I would be interested, and I waited for a few minutes until he was better prepared to depart for our short journey.

"Many tourists come here and ask us for rides in our gondolas," he responded after inquiring which country I was from. "For them, it is fun. For me, it is just what we do here."

The man operating the gondola that day took me on an extended loop around part of the city. Houses were built right along the canals, with water lapping at their sides as we glided past. The city is considered by some to be an architectural marvel. Several hundred thousand residents live here, and for them, to get from point A to point B, it is considerably faster to jump into a boat or gondola instead of jostling about the crowded streets which are most times filled to capacity with tourists. The city is one of the most-visited cities throughout Europe.

Venice is comprised of more than one hundred islands and nearly one-hundred-fifty canals. Throughout the city, you will also find more than four-hundred bridges, many of them small foot bridges that provide access to pedestrians and bicyclists.

During its genesis, buildings within the city were constructed by utilizing long wooden piles which were driven up to sixty feet into the ground. By digging so deep, the piles would reach a desirable footing which reached past the weak silt and soils. The hard clay which is located far beneath the surface of the city streets, provided an adequate stability for the earliest buildings which were built here.

Although the wood which was used throughout the earliest construction of these buildings was quite water resistant, the piles, over decades, slowly began to deteriorate due to their constant companion—the restless waters of the canals.

Prior to entering the city of Venice via train, we passed over a lengthy bridge. Venice is largely surrounded by water, and building experts say that the city has been sinking slowly throughout the past few decades. Sea levels have changed here as well, and the city has become increasingly prone to flooding. A few years after I visited Venice, the city suffered devastating damages due to historic flooding, which rose to dangerous levels inside shops, restaurants, and residences.

However, once outside the city, while returning to mainland Italy, passengers on departing trains will see pastoral communities and verdant fields and meadows. Sheep and other livestock are abundant in Italy, and rarely is a meadow seen unoccupied by livestock.

Vineyards are also quite plentiful here since the country produces a considerable amount of wine. In fact, it is suspected that some of the oldest wineries in the world are located here. The country also is one of the largest producers of wine throughout the world, with nearly two million acres under vineyard cultivation. European countries such as France, Italy, and Spain produce nearly fifty percent of the world's wine.

There is a saying which many folks repeat that suggest that a glass of wine within some of these countries is cheaper than a glass of water. However, I do not know whether this is accurate or not, since I didn't compare the prices of the two beverages while I was visiting those countries.

Majority of hotels throughout Europe are small and unique. An unsuspecting tourist might even be surprised to learn that most of the small hotels do not have elevators. Some do, of course, but many others rely on the physical energy of their hearty guests to transport them to their rooms, sometimes at the expense of walking up four flights of stairs.

Throughout my travels to Europe, I came across an exceptionally tiny elevator that was located inside a budget hotel. The elevator was so small that I had initially wondered, upon gazing at the tiny compartment of the elevator, if I would need to send my luggage up the elevator by itself while I walk up the stairs to meet it as the elevator door opened. I'm really not sure if two grown adults would even have been permitted to occupy the elevator simultaneously.

Another interesting concept surrounding lodging here in Europe is keys. Throughout the United States, it is not uncommon to receive plastic key cards, which are often swiped or tapped on the doors of the hotel rooms. I saw very little of those key cards being utilized while in Europe. Instead, actual keys were often distributed to guests.

I did most of my European lodging in older, sometimes family-run businesses, and in most cases, these establishments had not updated to using cards as room keys. Turning the key to a hotel room created the sense of ownership, almost as if I were turning the key to a house which I owned. I believe that turning a key versus swiping a plastic card at a door is decidedly more personal.

Most hotel rooms in Europe which I stayed at were also on the small side. They were simple yet served the purpose quite well. Since I had been traveling solo, there was really no need for an impractically large, lavish room. Bearing this in mind, I had chosen to sleep in several budget hotels in Europe for that reason.

These smaller establishments that I chose also provided me with an opportunity to appreciate the authenticity of genuine European culture, an experience which is often lost inside the expansive corridors of a chain hotel.

Once, while sleeping at a bed-and-breakfast establishment, I even had the opportunity to experience the authenticity of the European rain from inside my room. This memorable experience came courtesy of a suspected leaking roof. After the water dripped on my pillow, I moved the bed a bit, so that I could sleep without being disturbed by the sporadic dripping. That night, I vowed that I would permit myself to spend a little more money on my hotels from that point forward.

Regardless of how interesting some of the rooms were, I was always glad for the safety which they offered me. It certainly beat sleeping outside in the dead of winter in an unfamiliar country. Even though most people throughout Europe greeted me with measurable hospitality, I was happy that I didn't need to sleep out on the streets, since I suspect that a tourist such as myself might have been an easy target for a person with less than honorable intentions.

A gondolier navigates his craft and passengers along the Venetian canals in Italy

Cathedrals, shops, and houses are all located along the Venetian canals

Colorful watercraft assists in transporting tourists and residents to different areas of the Italian city

Many residences and shops are primarily surrounded by canals

Narrow canals span the waterlogged city of Venice

The oar, handled by a gondolier, is seen from a seat of the watercraft

Tourists delight in riding in large watercraft such as the one which is seen in the distance in this photo

Small boats pass under bridges hundreds of times throughout a typical day

Small foot bridges are located throughout the city of Venice, which connect pedestrians to nearby streets

The gondolas are extravagant and flamboyant

CHAPTER 6
ILL-TIMED AVALANCHES AND REVISED ITINERARIES

As the train snaked high along the mountainsides, I glanced out the window onto the expanse of the snow-covered valley below. The moon shone softly, casting a gentle glow across the valleys of Switzerland. In the distance, the lights of a quiet mountain town twinkled in the cold of the winter night. The lights seemed to burn brightly, like lit embers against the wintry, snowy backdrop.

A few feet of fresh snow had blanketed the region earlier that day. From my window on the train, I could see that a string of moving lights glistened in the far distance. I observed them for a while before concluding that they most likely belonged to another train that was slowly navigating its way along the opposite mountain range. That train, in much the same manner as the one which I was occupying, was probably loaded with passengers and tourists eager to catch their first glimpses of the mountain ranges of Switzerland. I wished that we had arrived throughout the daytime, since I would have been able to fully grasp the beauty of the region which we were traveling though. Still, the following day, I got to see my share of snowcapped mountains and other wintertime scenery which Switzerland is known for.

Before we arrived at the Zurich train station that night, our train followed the mountain ranges for approximately an hour or so. Sheer drops consisting of thousands of feet were mixed with dizzying twists and turns. We also passed through occasional tunnels, which always appeared quite narrow, barely providing adequate wiggle room on either side of the train. For example, I would not have wanted to place my arms between the train cars and the sides of the tunnels.

After twisting and turning, our train finally arrived at the over-zealous Zurich station. This station was one for the books. With forty-four platforms, it was no wonder that I was confused upon exiting the train. It seemed each floor of the station had more tracks and escalators than the previous one had.

Amidst the confusion, I managed to find my way out of the labyrinth of platforms and waiting trains. My exit wasn't a well-thought out strategy; it might have instead been a stroke of luck. That evening, instead of taking a taxi, I walked slightly more than one mile to the hotel where I had reserved a room just a few hours earlier. The night was indeed quite cold, and the biting wind chill made for a brisk walk.

The city was largely void of traffic, so the journey to the hotel was a rather peaceful one and provided me with a time for reflection as well as an opportunity to plan the events of the following day. My time in Switzerland would be limited, and I was aware that I would need to prioritize my time if I wished to see all the attractions that were on my agenda. The next few days would be filled with an abundance of mountain scenery, or so I had hoped.

But things don't always go as planned while on vacation. Due to an intense snowstorm which dumped an additional two feet of fresh snow on the area throughout the night, the train ride which I had scheduled the previous day was incapable of traversing through the Alps at that time. I had been concerned about this and had done my share of worrying the night before, as I anxiously watched the weather radar. Indications were quite strong that a powerful winter storm was headed right for the area that I was staying at.

In efforts of alleviating my anxiety and attempting to be a proactive tourist, I hurried to the front desk of the hotel, where I approached the concierge and shared my apprehensions. "Will my bus still be able to take me to the train station tomorrow?" I anxiously asked the lady who was standing behind the check-in counter. Not even waiting for her response, I quickly added, "The forecast is calling for two feet of snow tonight," in hopes of providing an explanation for my inquiry.

The lady smiled warmly and said matter-of-factly, "This is Switzerland, the bus will come pick you up even if it snows three feet tonight."

With an air of confidence, I accepted her response and headed for my room. I slept soundly that night, not knowing what lay in store for me the following morning.

The next morning, after a restful sleep, I glanced out the window. All that I could see was a wall of snow. It was everywhere. A group consisting of five men were busy shoveling snow from around the cars in the parking lot. Wielding shovels, blowers, and elbow grease, the crew freed each car one at a time while I watched for a few minutes. I didn't wish to be late for my arrival at the train station, therefore, I quickly ate breakfast before boarding the waiting bus which took me and several other tourists to the nearby train station. As promised, the bus had arrived on time that morning. However, the train line was inoperable due to heavy snow.

Of course, this news came as a disappointment. I expressed my dismay while I stood at the ticket counter, but the attendant assured me that there was nothing they could do. "There is heavy avalanche activity along your route," was the explanation. "The train cannot pass through. We have workers who are attempting to clear the tracks, but, unfortunately, additional avalanches are occurring ahead of their location as well."

Not sure of what my next step should be, I asked if there are any tracks that are open and not within the avalanche-prone zones. "You could board a train to Italy," the attendant responded. I groaned a little, since I had just traveled from Italy the previous day and did not necessarily wish to return under these conditions. "It might be your best option, unless you want to stay around town and wait until tomorrow. The tracks which head into the mountains might be cleared by that time."

The attendants had seemed helpful. At least they were offering solutions, even though they weren't entirely desirable. But I decided that I didn't wish to mope around on an otherwise wonderful vacation, so I purchased the ticket for a train which headed into the opposite direction of my initial desired destination.

Do I stay in my hotel room all day and look out the window, or do I jump on another train that is headed in a totally different direction? I had asked myself before purchasing the ticket. It only took a few minutes of deliberation when I considered that in Italy, I could enjoy another slice of fresh, authentic pizza for lunch. It seemed like a logical and practical solution to my dilemma. Plus, I secretly suspected that pizza might make everything better.

A few hours later, the train arrived in a little mountain village in Italy, just in time for lunch. I was glad that I had decided to go, instead of sitting in my hotel room all day. Besides, it isn't every day that I have the opportunity of going to Italy for fresh pizza while being practically snowbound in Switzerland.

The following day didn't disappoint and appeared to be full of promise. The trains were able to leave the station. Early that morning, after purchasing my train ticket, I embarked on a thrilling eight-hour journey through the mountains. The journey was a visually stimulating one, and in some instances, around the sharpest curves, the train cars appeared to be precariously suspended along the extreme edges of the sheer mountainsides. As I looked out of the train windows, deep into the valleys below, I became a bit nauseated. The spectacular views were unlike anything I had seen before, at least in real life. Merely looking at pictures of striking scenery such as this never seem to do it justice.

In the valleys, clear, sparkling blue waters shimmered in the rays of the weak winter sun. The rippling waters glistened like diamonds while flowing effortlessly down the rocks into the pristine lakes below. Everything seemed to be much cleaner here in the Alps. The melting snow from the steady rays of the sun added to the consistent flow of water as it meandered and dropped from the jagged mountainsides.

It was easy to indulge in such visual beauty for a few days, and I became quite content to do so. Originally, my itinerary had suggested that I might only be staying in Switzerland for a day or two. Along my itinerary, the small mountainous country was going to be a quick stop over, on my way to other countries. Sometimes, a change of plans—at the hands of nature— is the best thing that can happen to a tourist.

A Swiss train approaches a tunnel deep within the mountains

A Swiss train leaves the station on its way to the mountain passes

A passenger train arrives at a station near Saint Moritz

Weaving seamlessly through the snow-covered valley prior to its mountain trek,
a passenger train glides through a winter wonderland

A village nestled deep within the plunging Swiss valley

A wintry scene captured through the lens of the author's camera from the seat of the train

Snow covered mountain peaks loom high above a village in Switzerland

An unusual delivery vehicle seen along the streets of Zurich, Switzerland

The train paused briefly atop the mountain somewhere in the Swiss Alps

High peaks provide a wonderful winter scene for passengers who travel via train along a mountainous route

Snow covered mountain peaks can be seen from the greener pastures in Italy

CHAPTER 7
SNOWBOUND VILLAGES AND RECONNAISSANCE FLIGHTS

The stillness and serenity of the Swiss mountain, as the light breezes whispered and tugged at the pristine snowbanks, was a scene which would not soon be forgotten. It seemed all so dreamy. Without creating as much as a sound, the electric powered train glided along the elegant curves which wrapped around the sides of the snow-covered mountain.

The *Glacier Express,* the passenger train in which I was thoroughly enjoying myself, operates an approximately seven-hour ride through the most majestic areas of the Swiss Alps. Throughout those entirely entertaining seven hours, the route consists of passing through more than one-hundred tunnels and traversing several dozen bridges of varying sizes.

Soon after I boarded the touristy train, I took notice of the sliding windows, which provided unrestricted access to the visually pleasing scenery. I quickly took advantage of this, thrusting my camera out the open window, hoping to get clean shots. The cold mountain breeze quickly found its way inside the train, and upon opening the windows, my lungs were filled with the fresh mountain air.

The window didn't stay open very long, however, since the force of the moving train seemed to push some of the powdery snow which appeared abundantly along the tracks, right into the large windows. The breezes picked up intensity from time to time, and a quiet spell was usually followed by an occasional gust of wind. The winds seemed to ebb and flow in much the same manner as the restless waters of the ocean do.

Occasionally, there were whiteout conditions atop the mountain when the winds blew with ferocity. Blowing snow intensified during such moments, sending snowflakes catapulting like stinging needles through the atmosphere. This effect usually resulted in me losing sight of our surroundings for a spell. However, the fleeting reprieves from the unobstructed views certainly provided my camera with a much-needed break.

The weather seemed to change quickly here atop the mountain. For example, the sun could be shining brightly and shortly thereafter, the train was plunged into a raging snow squall. During the height of a random storm, clouds of white powder billowed with intensity, crashing into each other as the lines between the sky and the ground became increasingly blurred. Whenever such an event occurred, it seemed as if the blanket of white was never ending. We were caught in several of these vortices for some time. But the train continued traveling deeper and further into the swirling white hurricane, blazing its way to the station as it dutifully climbed the last leg of its cold, frosty journey. Upon our arrival, I gathered my belongings and prepared for disembarkation.

Throughout the eventful journey, we had passed through some high elevation areas that had been inundated by over twelve feet of snow. That is a considerable amount of white powder. It had been exciting to observe the beauty and ferocious intensity of winter, as well as experiencing the powerful solitude of a calm winter day, all wrapped in one. That day, what had begun as a gentle journey had ended in a serious snowstorm. In Switzerland, this is not uncommon during the winter.

After the journey had concluded, I left the station and walked through the swirling snow for approximately fifteen minutes, fighting my way through the storm on my way to the hotel. Exhausted from treading snow, I smiled with relief when I stumbled to the front door of the hotel.

Later that evening, while sitting on the hardwood floor of my cozy room, I observed the storm as it continued to rage outside. Munching on fresh popcorn while watching the snow fall with urgency seemed like it might be an acceptable form of activity, so I trudged toward the hotel lobby. Many European lodging establishments provide their guests with complimentary treats, such as cookies, popcorn, crackers, or chocolates.

Getting to the small village of Zermatt, which is nestled in the foothills of the Matterhorn, was a real production. The following day, due to yet another ambitious snowstorm that flexed its muscular might across much of Switzerland, this time, my train was delayed for three days instead of only one. This news was less than desirable, of course, but somehow, I found a way to remain calm and in good spirits, despite the consistent disruptions to my itinerary which Switzerland seemed so interested in introducing me to.

When the mountainous train routes finally opened again after the extended delays, my train departed for the remote mountain village of Zermatt. After having tried unsuccessfully to reach the town for three days, it felt remarkably good to be on the move once again, instead of waiting in a hotel.

I had reserved a room in Zermatt several days before, when I had initially expected to arrive, but due to the storms and avalanche threats, my travels had hindered me from reaching the secluded, car-free village. The Swiss residents who occupied the same train car that I did, explained that the recent weather conditions had been unprecedented, even for this region of Switzerland, regarding the sheer measure of snowfall which had fallen throughout the past few days. A few unusually intense, consecutive winter storms had unleashed their mischievous energy upon the region, which resulted in tourists and locals alike being snowbound in Zermatt, with no way to leave. (This was also why I hadn't been able to travel to the village, due to route blockages).

As I later learned, had I spent an extra day in Italy, I would have become one of those snowbound tourists in Zermatt. The village is nestled tightly between prominent mountain ranges, and the only way to access the remote village is either by helicopter or train, since no roads lead to Zermatt.

The situation in Zermatt, regarding the snowbound tourists and locals, had become critical during the three days that the consecutive, mighty winter storms had stalled above the small village. Due to several days of heavy snowfall, the mountain town had been cut off from its main lifeline, the passenger train. The train not only provides a method of transportation—a way out and in—for the villagers, but it also delivers much needed supplies each day to the village.

In a previous paragraph I had mentioned that the village is car-free and can only be accessed via rail or helicopters. I imagine snowmobiles could also access the village, although I was told that the two primary modes of transportation to and from the village is by train or helicopter.

During the winter of 2018, a reported total of thirteen thousand tourists had become stranded for the duration of three days due to the unprecedented amounts of wintry precipitation which had enveloped the region.

This uncommon weather event was a major conversation piece on the trains, and many locals marveled at what had been taking place during the past few days. The situation had even raised the interest of American news networks, as they also reported on the snowbound village of Zermatt. The village caters to wealthy and affluent tourists from all over the world, and the region is revered by adventure-thirsty backpackers and millionaires alike. I will let you guess which category relates best to me. (Hint, there was a backpack in my possession).

The day which I arrived in Zermatt, reconnaissance flights (helicopters) had been set in motion to assess the current situation of the stranded tourists. The town consists of less than six thousand permanent residents but can host more than fifteen thousand tourists within the dozens and dozens of lodges and hotels which are located within the village.

Due to the elevated risk of avalanches, the train lines were shut down, therefore, a chorus of helicopters had been deployed to evaluate the situation. The highest avalanche risk—a level five—had been confirmed that day by the Swiss government, therefore any hiking and skiing around the village was strictly forbidden. These announcements were made on our train while we were heading for Zermatt.

Once we were approximately halfway at our destination town (Zermatt) we were told that another avalanche had occurred and was currently blocking the railway a few miles ahead of us. The train attendants informed us that due to this unexpected disturbance, we would need to disembark at the next town—approximately a two-hour traveling distance from our desired destination—and quickly set up accommodations for alternate lodging that night.

This announcement appeared to displease majority of the passengers greatly, but as time passed, they seemed to have emotionally prepared themselves to disembark at the next station since the route had become inaccessible to avalanche activity.

Half an hour passed before the conductor made another announcement. "Our workers have been scrambling to open the line for us," the conductor remarked. "They have been using various explosive techniques and heavy machinery to remove the excessive amount of snow on the tracks in front of us. If the situation there continues to evolve in a positive manner, we could continue on our journey to Zermatt after all." Upon the declaration of this joyous message, the train's occupants, including myself, smiled with delight.

You would think this is where the roller coaster train ride should have ended, but it did not. After traveling for some time, approximately twenty or so miles close to our destination of Zermatt, the conductor made yet another announcement. This time, his tone was quite different.

"For those of you who wish to travel on to Zermatt, a helicopter will be required to transport you the final leg of the journey. Our team of men has been unsuccessful at opening the route which leads to Zermatt. Therefore, you will need to be flown in a helicopter to your destination village."

The demeanor on the faces of the passengers changed quickly from relaxation to excitement, with also a detectable measure of anxiety mixed in. There were probably less than a dozen passengers, including myself, who wished to travel on to Zermatt, regardless of the mode of transportation required for the final leg of our beleaguered journey. The bulk of us agreed that we would pay the small fee—seventy-five dollars each—to be airlifted to the village.

Upon arriving at a station where we would be scheduled to occupy the helicopters, I quickly took notice of the commotion around us. Helicopter blades were busy shredding the clouds as the pilots evacuated scores of people and delivered fresh supplies of food and bottled water to the embattled village of Zermatt. By this time, we were just outside the village—less than five miles away.

Portions of the roadway outside the train station were blocked by massive trucks which were loaded with critical supplies, which were destined to go to Zermatt via helicopter. I watched intently for a few minutes as the choppers lifted baskets of items right off the backs of the supply trucks. It was impressively efficient, and I had wished that I could have observed for much longer.

The whirring from the cavalcade of helicopter blades continued to buzz around in our ears as we walked into the tiny train station of Tashce, a small village located mere miles from Zermatt. Upon entering the station, one could not miss the throngs of media crews which were in place, eagerly filming the chaotic scenes inside and outside the station. By mere observation, you would be forgiven to assume that a major catastrophe had just occurred, and in a way, I guess it had. The moment seemed to be quite emotional for many, and dozens of people could be seen laughing and crying, when the station attendant announced that no one would need to pay for a helicopter ride after all; the avalanche crew had managed to successfully clear the tracks.

By this time, I wasn't quite sure what to believe or what to think. I felt torn. But mostly, I had looked forward to that helicopter ride. However, it was also wonderful to hear that we weary travelers were finally permitted to continue upon the last leg of our journey.

Upon our tumultuous arrival, the cheery snow-enveloped village of Zermatt, which was nestled neatly at the foot of the Matterhorn, greeted us warmly. I was glad to have finally arrived, even in the midst of high-drama and boundless chaos.

Heavy blankets of fresh snow covered the streets here, since locals reported that more than five feet of snow had fallen prior to our arrival. Up until that day, I probably had never seen that much snow at one time, in my life.

The scenes which unfolded in Zermatt were quite memorable. A handful of hearty tourists were skiing and snowboarding along the streets, while frequenting a host a fine restaurants and ritzy boutique shops. Several people had even utilized a toboggan and were navigating their craft, with equal amounts of skill and laughter, along the steep, snow covered streets.

A bird flies lazily in the wintry skies above Zermatt

A pristine scene outside the village of Zermatt

A wooden fence reaches the breaking point in Zermatt

Brightly painted houses provide a much needed respite from the continual white landscape

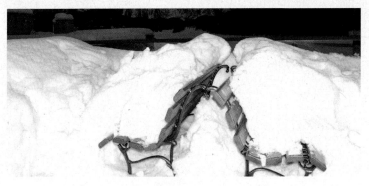

Benches are weighted by a heavy burden of fresh snow in Saint Moritz, Switzerland

Dramatic scenes, not unlike this one, remain etched in the memory banks of most tourists who visit Switzerland

Majority of tourists are enamored by the charm which Zermatt so easily exudes

Mountain peaks seen through the windows of a train car

Mountain peaks protrude in the distance as a sleepy village appears undisturbed by the passing train

Mountains surround the well-known holiday spot of Saint Moritz

A bicycle sets high atop a snowbank in Zermatt

Most days throughout the winter months, the tip of the Matterhorn,
one of the most famous mountains in the world, is shrouded in dense cloud cover

Occasionally, avalanches pose a threat to villages

Roofs are required to withstand a heavy snow load in Switzerland

Vehicles such as these, which operate solely on alternative fuels, are seen throughout Zermatt

Snow is everywhere in the avalanche-prone village of Zermatt

Snow is piled high in every available corner in Zermatt

The sounds of the village were heavily muffled by the thick blanket of snow

Water flows freely, dividing two streets, in the mountain village of Zermatt

Windy conditions prevail atop the mountain peaks

Winter lovers revel in the cold and white wonderland

Zermatt village, built right along the feet of the dominating Matterhorn

Zermatt, Switzerland, shortly after receiving a heavy snowfall

Zermatt was transformed into a winter wonderland by a heavy storm the day before the author arrived

CHAPTER 8
GLITTERING CITIES AND DREARY DUNGEONS

As our train chugged along the mud bogs and swamps of the Czech Republic, we also occasionally passed by some farming communities. Throughout the five-hour journey by rail, our worn-out, east-European train cut across a swath consisting of thousands of acres of farmland and wetlands.

Along the journey, it was fascinating to see a familiar sight; two *John Deere* tractors in operation in the heavily saturated Czech fields. A smile tugged at the corners of my mouth as I thought of at least a few friends back home in the United States who would be so proud to see these iconic green and yellow machines hard at work in the fields here.

There were distinct differences between the citizens of eastern Europe and the folks living within the regions of western Europe. As I observed the people of Poland and the Czech Republic, I took notice that they were quite different from the Italians, who had dressed fashionably and seemed polished and sophisticated. Here, in eastern Europe, people appeared considerably more down-to-earth, and in some cases, probably quite poor. Even so, the Polish city of Katowice and the Czech city of Prague were both quite modern.

The eastern portion of Europe also possessed a natural beauty, much like the western regions, however, in the western areas, verdant farmland as well as sprawling cities welcomed me under generally sunny skies. Here, in the eastern half of the continent, dreary weather seemed to prevail. I reminded myself that I was, after all, traveling throughout the winter months, and less than exciting weather was probably in abundance at this time of year.

Perhaps one of the most random adventures throughout my time in Europe was when I decided, on a whim, to travel to the infamous Gravensteen Castle in Belgium. The Castle is more like a dreary dungeon, make no mistake, and it was within the walls of this Castle, as well as on its steps, that early Christians are said to have been tortured and killed for their faith.

As I was lying in my hotel room, approximately an hour away—by train—from the Castle, I became increasingly intrigued with paying this Castle a visit. A few moments before, I had discovered a pamphlet, intended for tourists just like myself, which pertained to information of the Castle. I quickly checked the train schedules and to my surprise, a train was leaving within fifteen minutes. I hurried out of my room and walked a block to the nearby train station.

That evening I spent a great deal of time walking around the immediate area of Gravensteen Castle. I had arrived thirty minutes after they had closed their doors for the day, and no indoor tours were available until the following day. Since I had already purchased a train ticket for another country for the following day, I thought it best to be content with exploring the exterior of the Castle, and the general area surrounding it.

The Castle itself looked formidable and foreboding as it stood there, brooding in the fading light of day. Vehicles were rushing about the streets within the immediate area and judging by the amount of foot traffic and cars, the Castle seems to have become quite the tourist attraction throughout the past few decades. Rumor has it that the town of Ghent, Belgium, was interested in dismantling the Castle during the early 1900s. However, due to public outcry, the Castle was permitted to stay, and instead underwent an extensive restoration.

Visiting the castle provided me with a glimpse of much-respected history regarding Christians who had been persecuted for their faith. The torturous methods and imprisonments weren't exclusively reserved for Christians, however, and others suffered greatly here, too.

I am told that visitors who are brave enough to venture inside the Castle walls can see an expansive collection of torture equipment, of which many of those dreadful instruments had been used during the thirteenth, fourteenth, and fifteenth centuries.

The history of this Castle reportedly dates to the Roman occupation. The current structure underwent a few additions and at least one major restoration project since it was originally built during the twelfth century.

Seeing the dungeon where dozens of humans had been imprisoned and tortured, and a few early Christians killed right at the site of this now tourist-infected Castle, was sobering and humbling. The Castle is surrounded by a moat and initially upon its construction, was a formidable sight to behold, I imagine.

What was once the scene of unspeakable pain and horrific human suffering has now been turned into a lavish playground for tourists who converge here from all over the world. Today, it is not uncommon to host weddings at the Castle. A few hundred years ago, unspeakable abuse occurred behind its walls. Now in 2018 (when I visited), the sight had become inundated by restaurants such as *Pizza Hut, KFC*, and *Subway*. Other fine dining establishments which cater to the appetites of a wealthier tourist, can also be found in proximity of the Castle.

As I cast the Castle one final glimpse before I walked away, down the cobblestone streets of the bustling, brightly lit town, I couldn't help but wonder what the city might have looked like and what its ambiance was akin to hundreds of years ago. Perhaps then, the streets were absent of laughter and good-natured conversations.

That evening, as I made my way to the train station, I stopped outside a large church which was located along the same block as the Castle was. Hundreds of tourists from many regions of the earth filled the streets. Surely, the town had found a way to distance itself from its gruesome, intolerant past. However, in the distance, as the tower of the Castle pierced the gloomy horizon, a symbol of a darker time remained.

Traveling solo can be quite rewarding, however, it can also present a measure of loneliness from time to time. For example, when you are out exploring the exciting and different countries on your own, you have no one else to rely on when you find yourself in a troubling situation. There is also no one around to help you read a map, which I am not always the best at. Neither is there anyone familiar with which to share those jaw-dropping views with. Additionally, there is no one to commiserate with when a steady rain washes away your perfectly scheduled plans which consisted of a day of sight-seeing. There is also no one to disagree with, no one to tell you that they would rather not walk a mile to a certain location to see an attraction that they consider a waste of their time.

I guess after weighing the pros and cons of both scenarios, traveling with a friend or two can be very rewarding and memorable, while traveling solo can also provide a person with the same rewarding sense of memorable adventures.

Perhaps, when traveling solo internationally, a person of faith learns to trust God more completely, rather than relying on other humans as much. I believe that we all have the potential to travel to distant lands and unfamiliar countries safely, regardless if it is a solo expedition or if we are accompanied by a few friends or family members. Common sense needs to be applied in every situation, and practicality should be the rule of the day. Even so, things can, and do, sometimes go awry, which usually makes for more memories.

The stirring views of the mighty mountains which I had become so accustomed to during the first leg of my European journey, were soon replaced by the haunting castles of Belgium and the piercing spires which emerged high atop the buildings within the modern city of Prague. The city, with seemingly a thousand spires in its arsenal, was fun to explore on foot, even though snowflakes fell from the dismal skies for majority of my visit.

However, much like any other city, Prague appeared to have its areas where one would do well to avoid. It was here in this city, that I felt the most uneasy being an American tourist. The streets were noisy and boisterous, unpredictable even, as reveling party goers mingled in the streets. Aware of my surroundings not a moment too soon, and wishing to remove myself from the seedy part of the city which I had obviously stumbled into, I caught a spring in my step, as I hastened through the darkened alleyways toward the safety of my hotel room.

There is a particularly scary moment which occurred while I was in eastern Europe that I will quickly share with you. While walking down the dimly-lit alleyways of one of the poorer cities of Europe in the middle of the night while searching for my hotel room, it was a bit unnerving to hear footsteps approaching me from behind at a rather brisk pace. Instinctively, I picked up my pace and hoped that the person behind me failed to notice my quickened step. The footfalls of the person following me also increased, and I became alarmed when I heard the owner of those fast footsteps exclaim, "Hey, Americano!" in a loud, booming voice. Judging by the situation at hand, it looked as if things might not bode well for me in that dimly lit alley that night.

I turned around, trying to act brave and hoping the person doesn't detect my fear.

"You don't want to go down there," the man remarked. Then, not waiting for my response, he asked, "What are you looking for? Can I help you?"

I told him that I was on my way to my hotel, but apparently, I had taken a wrong turn somewhere.

As I later learned, my hotel was on the other end of the street much farther behind me. I don't know what all was in front of me in that alley, but I thanked the man for pointing me in the right direction. Later, I felt quite silly for having been so startled, but I guess when you are alone at night in a strange city and a foreign country, situations tend to appear more dangerous than what they might actually be.

Now here I was, walking the mischievous streets of Prague a few nights later, in a similarly uncomfortable situation. But in each scenario, I am fortunate to have survived my brisk walks back to the hotel.

That night, for only a moment, did I dare to stop and appreciate the grandeur of the Charles Street Bridge and Wencelas Square as I hurried along the rowdy streets of Prague before turning the corner to my hotel.

Many of you are familiar with the Christmas song *Good King Wencelas* which was first published in the early 1850's. Here in the Czech Republic, in the center of the city square, a prominent statue has been erected of the late King Wencelas.

As I passed by the statue, which was in proximity of my hotel room, I breathed a sigh of relief, since once again, I had arrived at my sleeping establishment in the dark of a European winter night, unscathed and grateful.

Heavy clouds blanketed the skies over Budapest as the occasional intense snow flurry deposited fluffy white flakes onto anyone who was venturing about in the streets. Here, tall buildings were in abundance once again, and more spires pierced the skyline, while the historic city was cloaked in a serene blanket of white.

Small fruit markets dotted the busy, snow covered streets, sharing space with iconic eateries such as *Burger King, Subway, and Starbucks*. I stopped at one of the fruit markets and purchased a bag of fresh citrus.

Sometimes, handling strange currency can be a profound learning experience. At least here in Hungary, I thought I had quite the experience with decimals. I needed Hungarian Forints—the currency which the country of Hungary uses—to pay my taxi driver, who had driven me several miles from the train station to my hotel.

My driver seemed hasty and perhaps a bit irate. Maybe he hadn't appreciated driving several miles on the snow-covered streets. He spoke English well enough, and was measurably helpful, but his impatience continued to raise my anxiety levels just a bit. Therefore, as he waited in the car while I hurriedly extracted 10,000 Forints from the cash machine, I realized that I had only gotten the equivalent of around thirty-two US dollars. After I returned to the driver and paid my fare, I was dismayed to learn that he had only left me with three dollars. You would think 10,000 of any currency would last through a typical weekend, but here in Hungary, it hadn't even lasted the night.

The following day, I walked around the city for a bit. The Danube River flows through the city of Budapest, and a fancy foot (and traffic) bridge spans the river, which connects the two parts of the city. Sometime during that afternoon, a local resident chatted with me for a while. He explained that before the bridge was constructed many years ago, the city had been split into two parts—*Buda* and *Pest*. "Now today, it is all one city. Now, we call it *Budapest*," he remarked.

As I walked over the bridge once again, I couldn't help but notice several homeless people who were lying on the cold concrete. One of the men coughed as he clutched his thin blanket a bit closer. Another man sat beside a cardboard box. Words were scrawled on the side of the box, however, since the written words were not in English, I was unable to read the message. My heart felt heavy for these people, and I hoped that they found a way to keep the chilly winter winds at bay.

A boat sits idly in the still waters in proximity to the Gravensteen Castle in Ghent

A water worthy vehicle provides tourists with a safe ride on the Danube River

A large bridge spans the Danube River

A misty fog envelops the city of Prague as pedestrians meander along the streets

Although eastern Europe appears less wealthy when compared to her more-affluent neighbors in the western European regions, nice buildings like these exist in Hungary

Another pedestrian walkway where displaced persons converge

Boats continually passed underneath these buildings in Prague, the capital of the Czech Republic

Displaced persons typically searched for pedestrian tunnels such as this one, where they chose to lie on the cold, wet pavement, sometimes without as much as a cardboard box

Elaborate places of worship were abundant in Budapest, Hungary

Gravensteen Castle in Ghent, Belgium. It is said that many early Anabaptists suffered greatly behind the walls of this aging dungeon

Gravensteen Castle, which has an exceptionally dark and turbulent past, was built–in phases–in the 12th century

Mass transit is nearly impeccable throughout majority of Europe

A fruit vendor in Prague displays product during a light January snowfall

Pedestrians walk along a bridge which crosses the Danube River in Hungary

The pedestrian entrance to the supercilious bridge in Budapest

Tall spires, emerging from Hungary's Parliament Building, pierce the gloomy winter skies

The Hungarian Parliament building in Budapest

The lights of Prague light up the gloomy winter skies

The rippling waters within the Danube River flow quietly as the Hungarian Parliament building,
one of the most highly detailed structures within Budapest, looms in the distance

CHAPTER 9
DAMAGING WINDS AND HOLOCAUST HORRORS

As I boarded yet another train for another country, I settled in my seat for the night. In Europe, only a few night trains still operate. For example, I was told that if I had been traveling through Europe more than ten years ago, I would have had many options for traveling from country to country throughout the night. However, now there are a limited number of trains that operate on lengthy, overnight trips which travel from one country to another. Majority of those trips are now taking place throughout the day (2018).

This time, I was denied the luxury of having a bed on the train. Therefore, I was left with the undesirable situation of trying to catch some sleep while sitting upright in an uncomfortable position. I was grateful that the cars were spacious and compartmentalized, and there was only one other passenger in the car which I was occupying that night.

The car would have seated eight people comfortably, so I took it upon myself to occupy four of those seats, choosing to lie down in pursuit of a restful sleep. Since I am a human and not a horse, I prefer to do my sleeping without standing (or sitting) upright. My best sleeping is typically done when my head is hitting a pillow at a comfortable angle. But that wasn't going to happen that night, since I did not have a pillow. Still, even though the night was filled with various interruptions, including the announcements of numerous terminal stops, we managed to arrive safely at my desired train station the following morning, not much worse for the wear.

While in Europe, I primarily traveled by train or taxi. The trains were generally punctual and tidy, providing me and the other passengers with a pleasant traveling experience. The fastest trains were of course located in western Europe while the slower, less upscale trains were prevalent throughout eastern Europe.

Prior to this trip, even before I had left American soil, I knew that I wanted to see Auschwitz-Birkenau in Poland. Ever since my friend Phillip Martin had traveled to Europe several years before I had, he had related in vivid detail of what his experiences had been like while visiting the historical site. I had been intrigued by his accounts.

I had suspected that visiting the Birkenau-Auschwitz concentration/ extermination camps would be quite moving and thought provoking, but I believe it was perhaps much more so than what I had initially anticipated. While walking slowly across the vast area of land that had been the site of unimaginable atrocities and such great human suffering, I arrived at the conclusion that there surely is no end to the evils of the human heart and mind.

I found the experience of visiting and occupying the same rooms and buildings where heinous acts which had been inflicted upon the Jewish people and others, to be an ultimately sobering and utterly chilling one. Seeing with my own eyes the concentration camps and gas chambers, villainous experimental hospitals, and crematoriums, was such a stark reminder of the horrors which a generation of people had endured. During the 1940s, Adolf Hitler's ultra-effective Nazi death machine had been incredibly driven and determined to systematically eradicate the Jewish people and their faith and any others which were deemed undesirable and unworthy of life, from the face of the earth.

A heavy snow was falling the morning of my visit. The overcast skies were a perfect fit for the general ambiance of the solemn grounds. There were perhaps a few hundred visitors on the grounds, while only a handful of them were seen speaking, so somber was the moment. An unsettled sense seemed to envelop the property. Many of the visitors observed the artifacts with tear-filled eyes.

That day, having the opportunity of walking the same soil as a free man where so many before had suffered so greatly and had experienced such great personal loss, seemed truly inconceivable. The full measure and extent of human suffering which took place here is probably incomprehensible to most of us.

The historical site is considerably thought provoking, and as I glanced up at the pale afternoon sky bearing its winter chill, I wondered how many imprisoned souls had cast their dejected eyes toward the same sky so long ago, searching for an answer to their pleas for deliverance from their hopeless surroundings.

I continued to walk for several hours around the concentration/extermination camps, trying to imagine what it must have been like to have been forced into labor here without adequate food or care. Scattered across the property were dozens of large buildings, which had served as labor and/or death camps for Jewish prisoners and anyone else who was perceived an enemy of the Nazi agenda.

While there were other concentration camps throughout Poland during the Nazi regime, Auschwitz-Birkenau is the site of the largest of such camps. It is said to have opened during the spring of 1940. The property had reportedly been the site of a former military base.

I cringed as I walked through several buildings, which were once bathhouses where untold numbers of people had been gassed, their lives so viciously taken from them. The thought was horrific. Equally as unsettling was stepping into a building and seeing several crematory ovens, where the bodies had been reduced to ash. What really unnerved me was visiting the hospitals, where experimental horrors of all kinds are said to have taken place.

Most estimates calculate that between 1.1 and 1.5 million people died here at the Auschwitz camps; the vast majority of those killed were Jews. It is also estimated that the Nazis killed more than ten million people, six million of them Jews.

Much more could be written about the horrible history of the largest mass-murder site in the world, however, if you are interested in learning more about this subject, you will need to read another book.

In Lithuania, there is a unique place that is called the Hill of Crosses, which I would have really liked to visit. I nearly bought a train ticket to Lithuania, however, after contemplating on the number of days which remained on my itinerary, I decided it simply wouldn't fit into my timetable. Therefore, I will choose to merely share information with you which pertains to the site which I had so greatly wished to see.

The *Hill of Crosses* is located just outside the Lithuanian city of Siauliai and reportedly contains more than 100,000 crosses, of which most are dug into the sandy earth and placed there. It has been said that nowhere else in the world can you currently see as many crosses in one spot.

Since its genesis, the hill has become a bit of a pilgrimage for people all over the world, as they travel far and wide to place their crosses on this spot. Many believe that the first crosses were placed there by the families of rebels who had been killed in the uprising of 1831. However, it was only until 1863 that the crosses are believed to have begun accumulating significantly.

During Soviet rule, the erection and display of crosses on this hill was forbidden, and the site was reportedly bulldozed more than three times during the era of Soviet domination. The hill itself became a forbidden place, but even under this new stigma and threat of legal punishments, people continued to sneak to the hill during the night, under the cover of darkness, to place their crosses on this storied hill.

The Soviet army also reportedly burned all the wooden crosses on several occasions, and crushed the crosses that were made of concrete, using the powder of the crushed crosses to pave highways. The more earnestly that the crosses were removed and destroyed by the Soviets, the more fervently people continued to inundate the hill with their crosses.

While in Germany, I learned that Americans aren't the only nationality with a penchant for protesting. A protest had formed just outside my hotel room in Berlin one night, and several police vans were there and officers wearing riot gear stood at the ready, poised for action, should thing go awry. Approximately one-hundred-twenty people had formed in the city square, demonstrating their dislike for something the German government was up to. The night was noisy, as this demonstration took place less than five hundred feet from my room. The following morning, as I walked to the station to catch my train, broken glass littered the area.

Visiting the city of Berlin, the former headquarters of Hitler's Nazi regime, was also interesting, at least from a historical perspective. I went to the site where the Berlin Wall used to stand before it had been destroyed. This is also now a huge tourist attraction. The way in which I understand it, had I been standing on the wrong side of the wall just a few decades ago, my life would have been in grave danger.

The central train station in Berlin is really something to see, too. It is built five floors high, with platforms on each level. A large shopping mall is built around the station, and trains arrive and depart every few minutes, with arriving and departing passengers converging mere feet from the entrances of the large department stores.

During the time in which I visited the German city of Berlin, most of Western Europe was being ravaged by ninety miles-per-hour winds. The rare winter storm was dubbed a cyclone, and from what I gathered, this intense weather event doesn't take place every year. While it raged, the storm had killed four people in the Netherlands, just one day prior to my scheduled arrival in Amsterdam.

This weather event obviously disrupted train travel significantly, and my train from Berlin to Amsterdam was delayed two days, due to downed power lines and major disruption of service along the long-distance routes between the two countries. There was nowhere for me to go, so I retreated to my high-rise hotel as the storm raged outside. Occasionally, I glanced out the massive glass windows of my room, which served as a stark reminder of how scary it is to see big trees seemingly bend to the ground during the height of a ferocious storm. This storm packed quite a punch and claimed the lives of several people across three European countries until it had dissipated.

While there seemed to be much storm activity throughout my time spent in Europe, you should know that it wasn't always stormy. There also were pleasant days, which featured abundant sunshine. However, the sun shone no more than six days out of the thirty-three days while I was on my European journey. Perhaps I should have listened to the advice of a few friends—they had suggested that I wait to travel to Europe until summertime, when the weather is sunnier and inclined to be less volatile.

I don't regret having traveled during the off-peak season, since I don't find the idea of battling throngs of tourists appealing. Considering that sixty-seven million Americans traveled abroad during 2016, it is a probably a good idea to try to avoid such swarming crowds of humanity.

A building which was said to have been destroyed by Hitler's forces

A distant shot of the large museum in Poland

A somber scene of a concentration camp at Auschwitz-Birkenau

A train car, which once transported prisoners, stands idle now

An aged guard post on the compound

Columns protrude into the solemn winter skies

Most of the ruins appeared in a haphazard manner throughout the property

Aging structures which once served as medical facilities at the compound

Buildings such as this one typically housed prisoners

Flowers are placed at a wall where many prisoners, Jews and others, were executed.
This is where the execution-by-rifle took place

Dozens of buildings like these were strategically built throughout the compound

Many guard shacks, which were used on the compound during the early 1940s, occupied the property

Majority of the compound was surrounded by fences

One of the large medical buildings which were used during Hitler's reign of terror

One of many enclosed guard shacks on the property

Furnaces, which were once used for heinous purposes, still remain at the museum grounds today

Tableware is stacked in a corner of the museum

Photo taken at the far corner of the sprawling property

Piles of ruins prevail on the expansive compound

Rough sleep quarters were the site of many a sleepless night for the tormented prisoners

The bath house, where hundreds would be lined up for occasional baths

Prisoner uniforms are displayed at the museum

The gloomy skies seemed to match most of the visitors' mood when the author toured the compound in 2018

Visiting this site makes one wonder of the unfathomable despair which was permitted to blossom (albeit temporarily) here.

Some buildings were destroyed intentionally, while others fell in disrepair

The infamous words atop the metal gate seem to mock, even today

The property is expansive and requires several hours to walk to the various sites

The visitor entrance to the concentration camps in Poland

Train tracks, now largely in disrepair, run right into the main area of the camps

Unspeakable crimes against humanity took place in this building during the early 1940s.

The museum at Auschwitz-Birkenau

The museum, seen from a distance

Katowice (Poland) is a modern city located not very far from the aged concentration camps

Not every place was somber in Poland. Here, holiday lights cheer the city streets of Katowice

The central train station at Katowice is bedecked with holiday color

CHAPTER 10
TUNNELS, TRAINS, FERRIES, AND BICYCLES

The windstorm which had caused significant damage to the electrical lines along many of the long-distance train routes from Germany to the Netherlands, eventually relinquished its fury. This permitted the utility crews with critical time to rectify the situation. Meanwhile, millions of passengers remained stuck; with the only way to travel to the Netherlands via a bus, car, or airplane.

By this time, I was beginning to wonder why most of my routes seemed so prone to ailment. First, I was snowbound for several days in Switzerland, and now, Germany and the Netherlands seemed to be at odds with each other.

In Berlin, after having waited out the storm for two days, I approached the ticket counter at the train station early one morning. The sight inside the station was one of great dismay. Two lines weaved through the expansive, five-floor station. Literally, thousands of passengers had been awake much earlier than I had been, hurrying to the station in hopes of eluding the throngs of passengers who would undoubtedly inundate the station as they requested changes to their itineraries.

Reluctantly, I stepped in line behind many others. It was slow going, and a few of the escalators had been shut down, providing people the opportunity of standing on them while they waited to exchange their tickets. Behind the folks on the escalators, the line of weary ticket holders extended to the lower floor. Yes, the lines of people not only weaved through the majority of the floor space of the station, it also wound around the inside of the building, with people waiting on the lower levels to exchange their tickets on the upper levels of the station, where approximately fifteen ticket attendants worked feverishly to exchange/assist the ticket holders who needed to change their itineraries due to the storm event which had just taken place.

After waiting in line for more than one hour, one of these helpful ticket attendants called out my number. I walked up to the counter and explained my situation. "I am wanting to travel to Amsterdam," I explained. "I have been delayed two days now.

Will there be any trains heading that way today?"

The ticket attendant punched a few keys on his keyboard and glanced at his computer screen, frowning and then sighing. "Doesn't look that way," he replied apologetically.

"But I must get there," I reiterated. I didn't wish to remain in Germany for another day—or possibly even two.

"There is nothing I can do about these grounded trains," he explained. "The power lines are down between here and the Netherlands. Really, we can't travel there until the lines are back up."

"When do you expect that they will be repaired, and service restored?" I inquired.

"It doesn't look good; I will be honest with you. For the past few days, our country (Germany) has been refusing to repair the lines, saying that the Netherlands must repair them. Meanwhile, transportation officials in the Netherlands are saying that the responsibility of repairing these power lines along the train routes lies squarely on our government. Clearly, our countries are not getting along well at the moment."

Yes, it seemed that there might be an issue here which wasn't about to be resolved on its own. "So, do I have any options at all?" I asked him, hopefully.

"Yes, you do," he replied. "But you aren't going to like it. I could put you on a bus, which will take more than six hours to get to your destination," he explained. "But really, you don't want to do that. Those buses aren't comfortable like the trains are."

"I will take it," I replied quickly. "At this point, I don't mind sitting on a bus for several hours, if it gets me out of this city. I just need to continue on my journey, I can't spend majority of my time waiting here."

He quickly printed three different tickets for me, and while clutching them tightly in my hand, I was on my happy way once again. The bus ride wasn't nearly as bad as he had told me it would be. I found the thought of traveling to another country—even by bus instead of a high-speed European train—quite comforting to my adventurous spirit.

I arrived in Amsterdam (the Netherlands) late on a Saturday evening. After enjoying a late dinner, around ten o'clock, I feel asleep shortly after I returned to my hotel. The following day, I went exploring the city on bicycle. The preferred mode of transportation for many throughout Amsterdam seemed to be on the seat of a bicycle. Nearly all the hotels provided their guests with the opportunity of renting bicycles.

The people are exceptionally friendly in Amsterdam, and they love to ride their bicycles everywhere. Amsterdam, as well as a few other cities and countries throughout Europe, have established bike lanes which are reserved exclusively for bicyclists. I found the Dutch folks to be typically relaxed and easy-going people, but I did take notice of their impatience whenever I mistakenly ventured into the bike lanes while I was walking. This was apparently an intolerable situation for them, since they yelled and tooted their bike horns at me as they approached—if they caught me straggling in the bicycle lanes. Upon hearing their yells, I quickly jumped out of the lane. Pedestrians who straggle in bike lanes here just might be in danger of being run over with a bicycle.

By this point of the journey, my hair was beginning to look long and unruly, so, wanting to avoid appearing as if I were homeless, I searched for a barbershop while walking the streets of Amsterdam. My choices were varied, and I quickly settled for a shop that looked reputable. No sooner had I sat in my chair and was settled in for a nice trim, when I had a hair-raising experience and nearly jumped off the chair.

As the barber reached for a comb and his trimming set, I realized that neither of his utensils had been soaking in antiseptic. In America, it is customary that all combs and some select trimming utensils are soaked in antiseptic to stymie the spread of germs and viruses. I managed to calm my unsettled nerves and opted to remain seated like a gentleman—in contrast to my better judgment. (Fortunately, I didn't get lice, nor did I contract any illness that I am aware of).

There was an abundance of cheese and wooden shoes in the Netherlands. The smell of cheese wafted through the outdoor markets as I walked past the shops late the following evening. Wooden shoes were displayed in many of the front windows of the shops, in attempts of tempting a tourist to purchase a pair. They looked interesting, so I stopped at one of the shops and tried a pair. Walking was awkward, as you can imagine. You would not wish to take a pair of these shoes along on a hiking trip. Due to their weight and clumsiness, I chose resisting the purchase.

According to travel websites, the city of London, located in the United Kingdom, is among the most popular travel destinations within Europe. The modern city draws massive amounts of worldwide tourists each year. More than twenty million people reportedly visit London throughout an average year. Paris (France) is the fifth most visited city in the world (2018).

In order to reach the United Kingdom from western Europe, I was required to purchase a ticket for a train which travels through an underwater tunnel. Now, this tunnel is rather impressive, and while speaking with a train attendant, I learned some fascinating numbers regarding the tunnel and the trains which pass through it each day.

The trains which travel through the Channel Tunnel are referred to as the *Eurostar* trains. These trains are impressive and quite fancy and occupying one of them is like being seated in the lap of luxury. Everything from the lavish meals served on board to the seating arrangements have been carefully designed to cater to high-class businessmen and women who travel internationally between the UK and Europe—sometimes daily.

The train travels at speeds which reach more than 180 miles-per-hour, however, upon entering the Channel Tunnel, which transports the train underneath the English Channel, the train decreases its speed to just under ninety-nine miles-per-hour. The Channel Tunnel is thirty-one miles in length—that is the equivalent of more than one-hundred-sixty-eight Eiffel Towers stacked atop each other. Also, another notable point of interest—approximately twenty-three-and-a-half miles of the Channel Tunnel travels underwater, under the English Channel. This currently makes for the longest undersea tunnel in the world.

It was rather thrilling and unbelievable to pass through such a tunnel. I sincerely hoped that if the water decided that it wished to wipe out the tunnel, that it would do so after we had completed our passage through the tunnel. This engineering marvel of tunnels and train tracks which are underneath the English Channel is really something to experience. The train system here transports more than fifty-thousand people throughout a typical day.

For a very long time, I had wanted to be a passenger on this train. And now, my dream had come true. I smiled as the train cut through lush Belgium farmland at the beginning of our journey, before it transported us deep into the tunnel. The entire journey took less time than what I had expected, and we arrived in London in less than two hours from our starting point in Brussels, Belgium.

Prior to the construction of the Channel Tunnel, anyone wishing to travel between the two countries was required to endure a lengthy ferry ride. The building project first began in 1988 and was reportedly completed less than ten years later. Plans had been set in motion to build a tunnel such as this one long before the 1980's though, however, the ambitious idea had been put on hold for several reasons.

One report argues that the UK had feared a surprise attack from its enemies and was wary about constructing a tunnel that might inadvertently ease the facilitation of such an attack. According to one theory, it was agreed that sumps would be set into place, to allow each country (UK and Belgium) to flood portions of the tunnel, should a need arise for either country to protect itself from invading armies. (However, this information is disputed by a few other reports).

Prior to boarding the Eurostar, each passenger was subjected to similar safety inspections which are par-for-the-course in any international or domestic airport. For example, the passengers were required to place their belongings and luggage in an X-ray machine, and remove their belts and shoes, as well as remove anything from their pockets. As an added security measure, each passenger was required to walk through a full body scanner prior to being permitted aboard the Eurostar.

To remove the incredible amounts of earth and debris in order to build the Channel Tunnel, 580-ton machines were used to drill through the earth. The tunnel is the fourth longest used by rail passengers in the world and has the longest undersea portion of any tunnel throughout the world (2018).

The project of building the Channel Tunnel reportedly cost the equivalent of more than twelve billion Euros in today's money (2018). The actual completion cost was reportedly more than eighty percent higher than the initially expected construction cost. The average depth of the tunnel is fifty meters below the seabed, while the tunnel, at its deepest point, is seventy-five meters (more than 250 feet) below the sea level.

While London was rather disappointing in terms of what I expected, it was worth it to travel there—if only for the opportunity of traveling through the Channel

Tunnel. I walked around the city of London for a while, but quickly got bored, and traveled back to Belgium a few hours later.

In London, the British Library hosts many ancient artifacts and a plethora of rare books. The library is expansive, and is among the largest libraries in the world, in terms of the number of catalogued items. The library is estimated of having more than twenty-two million books in its possession. Some books, which are collected from many countries throughout the world, are exceedingly rare and date to 300 BC. Each year, the Library adds nearly a million books to its collection.

The St. Pancras International train station in London (United Kingdom) is a sight to behold. It took more than two decades to construct the expansive and lavish terminal. It is surrounded by bustling streets which are filled with thousands of pedestrians, deep within the heart of the city.

The lively London train station is said to be named in honor of a fourteen-year-old boy who was executed at the order of a Roman Emperor in the year 304 AD. After refusing to renounce his Christian faith, the boy was beheaded. Throughout an average year, more than thirty-five million people access the station throughout their travels.

While I traveled throughout Europe, I developed a fascination for railway stations. Therefore, I took it upon myself to do a bit of research on some of them. I discovered that the *Gare du Nord* station in Paris hosts 214 million visitors each year. (I guess I was one of them when I traveled there in 2018).

The *Roma Termini*, in Rome, Italy, sees over 150 million people from all over the world each year, while the *Cologne Central* station in Germany is occupied by a lesser number (102 million) of human beings who transit through its vast corridors. At a staggering cost of more than four billion dollars, the most expensive train station is located within the United States, in New York City.

Now I must begin preparing for my travels to Denmark, which will include a ferry ride. Once our train arrives at the ferry dock, the ferry will transport the train across a portion of the choppy waters of the Baltic Sea.

A public telephone booth, which once served an actual purpose,
now provides London tourists with a photo-worthy shot of times gone by

Most people living in Amsterdam own either a boat or a bike; some own both

A unique looking restaurant in Amsterdam

A bird appears undisturbed as bicyclists rush by, ringing the bells on their bikes,
in efforts of encouraging pedestrians to rush out of their way

Amsterdam Central train station. Majority of the time,
the most elaborate buildings throughout Europe were either cathedrals or train stations

Bicyclists have the right of way in Amsterdam; pedestrians must move out of the way for oncoming bikes. This is enforced.

Bike bridges are abundant throughout the city of Amsterdam

Buildings reflect perfectly in one of the many canals

A vendor has created a peculiar vehicle to transport his wares

Cheese flats are certainly not scarce in Amsterdam

Cheese shops are fancy and expensive in Amsterdam

Colorful sweets inside a shop in the Netherlands

Headquarters of the International Criminal Court in the Hague (Netherlands)

Iconic red buses roam the streets of London

A small car seen along the streets of Amsterdam

Mass transit units and pedestrians fill the streets of Amsterdam, in the Netherlands

London's Big Ben clocktower can be spied in the distance

Majority of bicycles here are not expensive

There are more than 900,000 bicycles in Amsterdam

Police helicopters (see upper right of photo) continually flew over the city for hours

Public transit is cheap and reliable throughout Europe. Currently, a few European countries are weighing the possibility of providing public transportation free of charge

The UK flag flutters in the wind high atop the tower

The headquarters were located along an unassuming side street in the city of Hague

The longest escalator the author has ever seen; at the London Underground

This was a common sight throughout the Netherlands. The country prides itself on being environmentally conscious

Thousands of bicycles are retrieved from the waters of Amsterdam's canals each year

Unique buildings are not uncommon in Amsterdam

Wooden shoes were often seen on the sidewalks close to shoe stores

The parliament building in London was undergoing repairs to its exterior in 2018

CHAPTER 11
LENGTHY BRIDGES AND SHORT VISITS

Traveling from Germany to Denmark was nothing if not interesting. Had you been with me, I imagine that you would agree. After punching my train tickets from Amsterdam to Berlin to Denmark, I realized that it is rather easy traveling from country to country within the *Schengen Zone.*

The *Schengen Zone* is a collective region consisting of twenty-six countries within Europe that have agreed to facilitate the ease of travel by opening their respective borders without requiring travelers to provide passports or other documentation while traveling throughout these countries.

After a lengthy train ride which began in Amsterdam and included several train changes, the conductor of the train which I was occupying, which was now just outside Denmark territory, announced that the train would be stopping for a few minutes. "We will be stopping briefly here," he announced. "We are now arriving the ferry that will transport us across the waters to Denmark."

At the time that he made that announcement, we were still technically in German territory. However, when I had purchased the long-distance train ticket, I had no idea that we would be traveling on a ferry at any point throughout the journey. You can imagine that I became a bit confused and somewhat flustered upon hearing such an announcement.

Still, at this point, I imagined that each passenger, including myself, would be required to disembark the train, grab our luggage, and then step aboard the ferry. But my assumptions were very incorrect.

"The train will be continuing onto the ferry shortly," the conductor announced after the train had stopped moving for a few minutes. "Once we have successfully navigated the train onto the ferry, all passengers will be required to leave their seats and step onto the upper deck of the ferry. You must leave you belongings behind. Do not bring your valuables with you. Leave them by your seat on the train."

This announcement was quite troubling to me—until he continued. "The train cars will be locked once everyone has completed disembarkation. No one will be able to return to the carriages until an attendant unlocks the doors. Due to insurance purposes, no passengers are permitted to ride inside the carriages of the train while the ferry is in motion. Thank you for your cooperation."

This was exciting, for sure. Upon this final announcement, my anxiety was stilled and peace of mind prevailed. I quickly left my luggage and valuables behind and trudged up the steps of the ferry towards the upper deck, where we passengers were supposed to converge and wait until the ferry had completed transporting us— and our train cars—across a body of water which connected to the Baltic Sea.

Once each of the passengers had left the train and made their way to the upper deck of the ferry, an attendant locked the carriages of the train.

While walking toward the stairs, I had taken the opportunity of becoming familiarized with my surroundings. On the lower deck, right beside our train carriages, were cars and trucks—many of them. The ferry was outfitted with rails on the lower deck, making it perfectly accessible for the train to drive onto it. Therefore, a lengthy commuter train, twenty tractor-trailers, and multiple cars easily fit on the large vessel.

After I reached the upper deck, I was curious how soon we would be leaving. Seeing ferry personnel close by, I walked over to one of them and inquired how soon the ferry would be scheduled for departure. The lady smiled warmly, and replied, "Oh, we have been moving for about five minutes now."

I was impressed. The ferry had been that remarkably smooth that I thought we had still been docked and sedentary.

The ferry consisted of several floors, and a vast amount of boutique shops were located on the upper deck. The shops were upscale and catered to the folks within the high-fashion industries. Luxury items of all kinds could be purchased aboard the ferry, most of these items were sold duty free. There was even a lively casino aboard the vessel. A sign posted at the center of the upper deck declared that a total of 1,140 people could occupy the vessel.

The duration of the ride consisted of approximately forty-five to fifty minutes. Throughout the journey, a few passengers, as well as myself, stepped out onto the deck of the ferry and breathed in the chilly sea air as we glided effortlessly across the choppy waters.

As we reached the conclusion of the journey, and our vessel began arriving closer to land again, the conductor announced that every passenger which had occupied his train, must now begin making their way to the train once again.

"Once the ferry reaches the shore, our train will continue to Copenhagen (Denmark). The train will leave promptly once we reach shore. Please find your seats on the train at this time."

As you can imagine, upon this announcement, there was quite a scurrying of feet as everyone descended two flights of stairs to their assigned train seats. No one wanted to be left behind on the ferry.

When the ferry reached land, the train simply continued its journey via the connecting rail system that was constructed on the ferry dock. After traveling for a distance, our train crossed a lengthy bridge that was simultaneously accessible to both trains and automobiles.

For the duration of eighteen kilometers (eleven miles), cars and trains occupied the bridge, passing by each other in fleeting fashion. This suspension/box girder bridge is known as the Great Belt Bridge, which transported us across another body of water.

More than twenty thousand cars travel on the bridge each day. Nineteen percent of Denmark's total border traffic crosses this bridge, and a total of twenty-nine thousand passengers cross the bridge daily, via bus, train, and private automobiles. There are many islands in Denmark, and it appeared as if the country is in no short supply of bridges. However, they may not have enough, since a project for a new bridge, which is expected to span nineteen kilometers from Germany to Denmark, has remained in a national discussion for the past few years.

The country of Denmark was an interesting one to visit. I especially enjoyed the vivid hues of the brightly colored buildings as their colors clashed effortlessly against the grey skies of winter, which seemed to dominate the region throughout my visit. Gentle breezes, floating along its canals, bore a distinct chill, and I was required to purchase an extra hoodie to brave the harsh wind.

My visit in Denmark was cut rather short due to the weather delays which I experienced in Switzerland and Germany. Therefore, with not much more to discuss regarding the country of Denmark, I will move us right along to Sweden, the next country on my itinerary.

Sweden is a beautiful country that has an abundance of captivating scenery. The country is not quite as cold as one might expect for Scandinavia. Neighboring countries such as Finland and Norway tend to be subjected to consistently colder temperatures throughout the winter.

A special memory which I hold close in my heart when my mind travels back to Sweden, is the night that I slept on a retired fishing ship, which had been repurposed to serve as a motel. The experience was unique and redefined my idea of spending the night on the waters.

Strategically placed along the shores of the Baltic Sea, this floating, docked motel served as my resting place for a night. Within the immediate area, several other old boats lined the harbor, extending a warm welcome to other overnight guests.

Walking onto the characteristic Swedish boats and finding my incredibly tiny room on the third floor of the docked, floating motel, was something I won't soon forget. The waters were restless, and energetic waves easily tossed the watercraft about with a gentle, consistent motion throughout the night. Still, I managed to keep sea-sicknesses at bay as the blustery, icy winds of the Scandinavian night howled around the corners of my floating refuge.

As I peered out the small windows of the cozy cabin, I observed the lights of the city as they twinkled and danced like sparkling diamonds across the restless waters. After watching the disquieted waters, I, too, became restless and energized, and decided to take advantage of the easily accessible city on foot. Late at night, I headed out into the dark in search of yet another late dinner at a café.

Two days later, it was time for me to move along to another country once again. I recall that it was with a reluctant heart that I bid farewell to Sweden, the land of friendly yet overly tall, blonde human beings. (And severely overpriced food, I might quickly add).

Regarding the tall humans here in Sweden, I felt a bit small and short when I took notice that even most of the women were taller than I was, which left me feeling like a small American boy in the midst of a sea of giants—friendly giants.

A commuter train travels across a bridge in Stockholm

The author slept in this watery, Swedish hotel on a windy winter night in 2018

At a train station in Stockholm, Sweden

Early morning light appears on the horizon in Norway

Denmark provided an abundance of interesting structures

Overlooking the restless waters on an icy, windy night in Stockholm, Sweden

Many boats, much like this one, were docked right alongside the narrow streets in Denmark

Photo taken from the window of the boat hotel where the author slept in Sweden

Fowl of various sizes gathered in the waters near Malmo, Sweden

Houses and shops appear somewhat haggard in Denmark's Old District

Colorful houses are a trademark sign in Denmark

Boats are a common sight along Denmark's various waterways

CHAPTER 12
NORWEGIAN NECESSITIES AND FINNISH FORESTS

A kaleidoscope of vivid imagery, consisting of brightly colored Norwegian buildings, served as a stunning backdrop to the pristine, white mountains which graced the landscape along the most scenic train ride within the country. Throughout an eight-hour journey, the train sliced through Norway's remote regions and occasionally permeated areas which consisted of small villages. The scenic route was quite reminiscent of the routes which traversed through the Swiss Alps, although the buildings which occupied the many valleys along this Norwegian route were considerably more colorful.

Fields of crystallized snow twinkled in the gentle rays of the late afternoon sun as we glided past in a seemingly effortless manner. Whenever the train ascended above the tree line, the amount of freshly fallen snow was substantially deeper to that which was seen in the lower regions and valleys. Above the tree lines, the temperature plunged as well, and within one hour the outside temperatures had dived from a cozy thirty-four degrees Fahrenheit to a frosty three degrees.

The beauty of the snow-covered Norwegian wilderness was memorable to witness. By the time the train ascended to the most picturesque portion of the route, majority of the tourists who occupied the train were standing up, staring out the windows of the train in disbelief at the beauty which their eyes beheld.

Norway boasts not only of raw beauty, such as what we saw here on our train ride, but also of modern engineering. Here, within this country, the longest car tunnel in the world is found, which spans twelve miles in length and features rest stops throughout to accommodate sleepy drivers. The drivers simply commandeer their vehicles to one of several neon-lit rest stops, which are located throughout the tunnel. The rest stops serve as an opportunity for the drivers to recharge their mental batteries, refreshing themselves before continuing along their journey.

Centuries ago, in the Land of the Vikings, many early farmers intentionally chose to live together in huddles of four or more, since this greatly provided them with the opportunity of sharing precious resources, as well as enhancing their overall sustainability. The early farmers learned to live and work together somewhat akin to small communities, not unlike the close-knit communities which the Old Order Amish and horse-and-buggy Mennonites are known for throughout North and South America.

After Christianity was initially introduced to Norway, following the ruthless rule of the Vikings and decades of persistent paganism, many people reportedly walked to Sunday services for the duration of several hours—sometimes four—to attend and worship in crude wooden churches. During that time, due to the rising popularity of Christianity, there was a significant lack of churches in Norway, and they were scattered between far distances. Historians believe that Christianity initially took hold here sometime throughout the twelfth century.

Waking up each morning with the only pressing issue at hand being where and what you want to see that day can quickly spoil a person. I was rapidly becoming aware of this. But I knew that this wonderful traveling experience would reach its conclusion all too soon, so I decided to enjoy it while it lasts. After all, there is really nothing like an open, loosely planned schedule while traveling. The flexibility of planning your own schedule can be a good learning experience—even when avalanches or heavy winds cross your paths.

During my European travels, I was occasionally approached by what appeared to have been temporarily displaced or homeless persons. I saw quite a few people who were sleeping on a crude bed of soiled blankets and broken cardboard. Their hair was typically tousled, and a dejected look could be detected upon eye contact. My heart went out to them, since majority of the time, I met these folks along the streets under the cover of darkness, as the cold of night began to settle, in earnest, onto the uncaring streets.

I couldn't help but wonder what string of circumstances might have occurred or had developed over the course of time which led these folks down the path of displacement? Were some of these people enslaved by their personal vices? Perhaps. Likely, a great deal of them were good people, who had simply made poor decisions at some point throughout their lives.

I personally made efforts to assist such persons whenever it seemed appropriate. For example, if someone had a physical disability or was significantly elderly, I gave them some money if they asked for it. However, far too often, young, able-bodied individuals approached me for money. This seemed a bit odd, due to the fact that they appeared to be competent enough to establish an attractive salary or snag a decent-paying employment opportunity. The details of their lives were of course unavailable to me, but, in retrospect, I wish I had helped more people, instead of walking past some of them.

It was within the Scandinavian countries and eastern Europe where I saw the most displaced persons. The repeated scenes of people lying along the sidewalks and in parks on the coldest of nights was unsettling.

My train had arrived at my desired terminal in Bergen, Norway around mid-afternoon. The clouds had settled in heavily as the day progressed, and by evening, a steady rain was falling. It was the type of rain that wishes it could be snow yet is denied the opportunity, due to the air being too warm to produce fluffy white flakes.

I should have gone outside for dinner earlier than I did, because now I needed to borrow an umbrella from the hotel manager or dash through the puddles which were fast presenting themselves. Not to mention the pelting rain which still fell with persistence.

Having eaten very little that day, I was persuaded—by the rumbling in my stomach—to abandon my warm cocoon within the high-rise hotel, and run a few blocks to the nearest McDonalds, in the rain. I arrived there only to discover that they had closed their doors approximately half-an-hour before I had arrived at the main entrance, looking and feeling very much like a miserable, wet person.

I quickly retreated my steps and purchased some snacks at the only other option that was available; the local 7-Eleven convenience store. Arriving at the hotel a few minutes later, I comforted myself by sitting close to the heater while I munched on my food. By the time I had finished eating the last cookie, my clothes hadn't dried completely, and they continued to cling to me uncomfortably.

Time kept ticking away and the days kept drifting by, in much the same manner as a high-speed train rushing along the European rails. Soon, it was time for me to leave Norway and head for another country. But now, for the first time since I arrived in Europe, I wouldn't be purchasing a train ticket. No, not even a bus ticket.

After much deliberation, I concluded that it would be best to skip going to Finland, since my itinerary seemed like it would not permit it. However, before I made such a weighty decision, I considered it might be a good idea to call a friend back home in the United States and discuss my options.

"You should probably make time for Finland, even if you don't think that you have the time to travel there by train. Why don't you consider purchasing an airplane ticket and flying there? I am afraid that if you don't visit Finland, you will always regret that you didn't go, considering how close you are to that country now. Besides, I recall you telling me how much you had looked forward to seeing the snow-covered forests of Finland," he had replied.

My friend Eric was correct. It would bother me if I didn't go to Finland, since I had looked especially forward to seeing that country during my travels. However, prior to leaving the United States, I had made a personal commitment—I would only travel overland while there—no airplanes except the ones which transported me to Europe and the one which takes me home.

I am glad that I permitted myself to deviate from that original plan. And I am also grateful for the encouragement of my friend who urged me to buy that plane ticket. The moments which I enjoyed in Finland were, without doubt, my favorite and most memorable of my entire European excursions.

A photo taken out the window of the train car early one winter morning in Finland

A train is retired near Finland's Arctic Circle

Steam billows from a factory pipe in Rovaniemi, Finland

The author saw more snow (in 3 weeks) throughout his Europe trip than he ever had before in his life

At a supermarket near the Arctic Circle

Cars can no longer park here due to Finland's excessive snowfall

The Arctic Circle proved to be quite snowy

Snow is piled high in the parking lot of a Finnish supermarket

A wintry scene along a narrow road in Finland

The snowbanks nearly reach to the lamp posts in Rovaniemi, Finland

The train station in Helsinki, Finland

The end of the tracks in the Arctic Circle, Finland

CHAPTER 13
A CACOPHONY OF CANINES AND ELUSIVE NORTHERN LIGHTS

Moments before the Norwegian plane which I occupied had touched down on the Finnish tarmac, I eagerly anticipated the experiences which might be awaiting me. I wanted to explore Finland in a thorough and exhaustive manner. Boarding a train which traveled deep into the forests appealed strongly to me. However, forests aren't the only type of scenery in abundance here—the country also has thousands of lakes.

For a country which is comprised of slightly more than 130,000 square miles, Finland certainly has more than its share of lakes—if the definition of lake pertains to a standing body of water. Up to 187,000 lakes can be found within the borders of Finland. The country's nickname *Land of a Thousand Lakes* is fitting, in part, yet also somewhat deceptive, since the country obviously has significantly more than one thousand lakes at its disposal.

Upon arriving in the capital city of Helsinki, Finland, it was rather easy to take note of the colder climate. Snow was falling gently as I walked along another street to my hotel. Majority of the time while I was in Europe, I was found trudging along the streets under the cover of darkness, since the daylight hours throughout most of Europe—especially in the northern regions—are greatly limited. The persistent gloominess was something to become acquainted with, however, I wanted to see Europe during the winter months instead of the summer, so I assumed that shorter daylight hours and gloomy skies were an essential part of the deal during this time.

The delightful winter adventures that Finland provided me were exhilarating and unexpected. The memories which were made within the borders of this cold and abundantly snowy country were nearly innumerable. I found myself wishing for an additional three days to explore even more of the culture here.

While in Finland, I enjoyed a two-hour dog sled ride which transported me through the snowy wilderness of the Arctic Circle. We will discuss that in greater detail soon, but let's first take a visual journey through the country via the scenic train route.

There isn't much that rivals or compares to an early morning train ride which introduces you to the vastness and beauty of a snow-enveloped Finnish forest. Gliding silently along the rails through the snowy forest just as dawn begins to break over the horizon was adequate motivation for me to peel back the heavy lids of my sleepy eyes. The scenes were worth waking up early for. For several hours that morning, I sat in my seat, rapt with attention, my face glued to the window as I visually indulged in the striking scenery of the snowy forests.

As the first peeks of daylight pushed through the clouds, I observed several Finnish farmers trudging through the heavy snow as they forged a path to their barns to care for their animals. Most of the farmers were carrying buckets, which I assumed contained food or warm water, as they made their way to the edge of their properties where small barns would wait in the early morning silence. As the train continued to slice through the snowy farmland, I took notice of a few horses that appeared spry as they eagerly nibbled on cakes of fresh hay that had been provided them atop a large snowbank.

The friendliness of the Finns was certainly something to take note of. I believe they were among the most hospitable people I met in Europe. The natives in Iceland also were very hospitable, and they just might receive the number one prize regarding friendliness. Throughout my journey, I met many wonderful and genial folks, however, not every country seemed to hold friendliness to a high standard. The least friendly and most socially withdrawn people that I met along the journey were located within the United Kingdom, primarily in the city of London.

Of the thirty-six cities that I walked through while in Europe, I felt the safest in Helsinki, Finland. Everyone, young and old, seemed so helpful and happy.

The train stations here were less crowded when compared to those in other countries, even though a steady stream of young and older folks filled the seats of the double-decker trains as they sought refuge from the sweeping arctic winds and walls of swirling snow which were so prevalent outside. It really seemed as if it was always snowing while I was in Finland and Norway, but I guess that is to be expected in January.

Finland's flag features a blue Nordic cross, which reportedly represents Christianity. The blue color also represents the country's thousands of bodies of water. The cross is set against a white background, which represents the vast amounts of snow which covers the land for the greater part of the winter months.

While traveling through Sweden, Norway, Finland, and Iceland, it was intriguing to learn that one of the reasons for the abundance of brightly painted buildings is to brighten the otherwise gloomy, sunless days of winter. The lack of sunlight and limited daylight hours requires the locals to find something cheerful and colorful, which cuts through the seemingly endless hours of winter drab.

My travels permitted me to remain in Finland for a few days. Here, the sun usually introduced itself around 9:30 AM, but it failed to climb high into the sky, instead choosing to slouch along the lower edges of the horizon. Most days, the sun had already set by 3:30 PM.

During one of the nights throughout my stay in Finland, I managed to brave the deep chill of an Arctic night and went in search of the Northern Lights. I walked for many miles to a spot where the hotel manager had told me that most tourists go to in hopes of catching a glimpse of the lights. "It is far, but I can call a taxi for you," he had offered.

I appreciated the gesture, however; the wind had stilled, and I anticipated walking to this spot on my own. It might seem more special if I were to reach this remote area outside the city of Rovaniemi without the aid of a taxi or local. Wielding a hand drawn map, I stepped outside the warm hotel and began my extended walk through the snowy, wintry world of northern Finland.

That night, the Arctic temperatures remained forbidding and frigid, even though the winds had subsided in a merciful manner. As I eagerly glanced at the skies in hopes of catching streaks of colorful light, it became obvious with each passing hour that the special moment which I had been longing for, might very well elude me.

I observed only a fleeting peek of the beauty of the Northern Lights that night, as I huddled behind a tree in an open area outside the city and away from the light pollution. Much to my dismay, heavy cloud cover dominated the night sky, and seeing less of the celestial wonders of the northern night skies was considerably disappointing to me.

The Finnish folks typically refer to the Northern Lights as *The Green Lady.* According to their legends, a green lady moves across the northern sky at night.

After a lackluster show of Northern Lights, it was time for me to begin my lengthy trek toward the twinkling of the city lights. Upon my return to the city, I had hiked nearly four miles in the Arctic cold, yet I still considered it to have been a worthwhile experience.

The following morning, I woke up at 4:00 AM to catch a dogsled ride. If you think that you might enjoy joining in the winter festivities, I encourage you to grab your heaviest jacket, gloves, and caps. The ride, I was told, will be intensely cold. (Turns out the people who had warned me about the cold had been correct).

After the early morning bus ride to the Husky farm had concluded, I arrived at the break of dawn at the largest Husky farm in Finland, where a host of other tourists and I would be receiving authentic dogsled rides through the Arctic Circle.

The deep voices of seventy-two rambunctious Huskies pierced the still, wilderness air and announced our arrival at the farm. The farm was located deep within the wilderness, and our bus was equipped with special tires and chains and a few other features, which permitted us to travel more effectively over the snow packed trails toward the property.

After a brief review of a few simple and practical rules and regulations concerning the safety and art of dogsledding, the instructor announced that we were now ready to begin our journey through the forest. I burrowed in the cold seat of my sled, bracing against the sharp wind that marched across the farm.

A team of a dozen personnel had worked diligently prior to our arrival to ensure everything was ready for our departure. I accompanied a tour group which consisted of approximately forty-five other guests, which hailed from various points of the globe. Each of us had been willing to brave the arctic cold, in search of the experience of a lifetime.

Each sled could adequately accommodate two persons. A musher always occupied the back of the sled, standing on the very edge of the sled as he navigated the dogs along the trails. Each sled provided a semi-comfortable spot for one seated passenger. A team of six Alaskan and Siberian Huskies pulled the wooden sled, transporting it and the passengers through the snowy wilderness.

I had the opportunity of operating a team of dogs for a while but chose not to. Instead, an energetic guest from South Korea was eager to conduct the navigation of our sled. I found it considerably more relaxing to sit on the sled and enjoy the breathtaking scenery, rather than attempt to wrangle with an unruly group of Huskies.

Upon our arrival at the farm, the dogs were full of life and rather boisterous. I was sure I wouldn't be able to handle them. But their energy levels began to wane noticeably as the journey progressed, and once the frisky canines had traversed the trails for an hour or so, they became more docile and manageable.

As the dogs made their way through the forests early that morning, their incessant barking reverberated through the wilderness as twelve sleds, pulled by dozens of hearty Huskies, glided across the snow packed trails. Even after running for more than an hour, the dogs maintained a decent pace, and ran surprisingly fast until they reached the end of the trail. The wind and snow blew in my face as we cut sharply around the corners of the trails, and on occasion, narrowly avoided tall pine trees.

Two hours of this delightful winter fun passed by too quickly, seemingly in the blink of an eye. All too soon, the journey had reached its conclusion, and we arrived, thoroughly chilled, at the owner's warm cabin which was located at the edge of Husky farm. Our host welcomed us with hot berry tea and delicious gingerbread cookies. While we enjoyed the treats and warmed ourselves by the fire, the owner of the farm expounded upon the various duties and responsibilities which are associated with operating a Husky farm.

I learned many things that morning regarding dogsledding. According to our instructor, the female dogs must always be the lead dogs. "It never works to have the male dogs lead the team," he explained adamantly.

"The strongest dogs are required to be placed in the middle of the team and the two dogs bringing up the rear need to be excellent followers. Each dog is trained for the duration of one year, while training generally begins at age one," he continued to explain.

Typically, each dog that receives training, graduates at some point in time. It is rare that a Husky can't be trained appropriately for dogsledding, however, some require additional time to be trained adequately and effectively.

The average life span of a Husky is between fifteen and sixteen years, the trainer remarked. Continuing, he added, "Our farm generally retires each dog once they reach the age of twelve. Each of the dogs that were involved in the sled rides this morning were raised on this property." The tour guide also mentioned that the proprietor of the farm owns more than three-hundred-thirteen Huskies.

During our dogsled adventure, we passed by dozens of reindeer farms in the northern areas of Finland. The unique animals were out on the snowy pastures, meandering about. It had truly been a vividly memorable experience to travel through the inhospitable polar region of Finland that morning on a sled which was pulled by a team of six ambitious, eager Huskies.

A cacophony of barking ensued shortly upon the tourists' arrival

A canine looks on as a team of dog sledders arrives at the camp

A few treks through the wilderness are conducted several times a day throughout the winter months

A canine perched atop a shelter in Finland

A canine resting after an early morning run through the wintry forests

Being transported on a dog sled through a wintry wonderland in Finland seemed to possess a sense of magical elements

A fire burns underneath the rudimentary shelter for the dog sled operators

A few of the Huskies appeared to possess icy blue eyes

A pair of canines nervously pace their kennel in Finland

A host of dog shelters occupy the forest floor in Finland

A trainer on a snow machine tracks the progress of the dog sleds

A snow fence is erected in Norway's mountain region

A team of dogs transport humans across the snowy, icy wilderness in Finland

A wintry scene in Norway's mountainous regions

An instructor attempts to calm the canines prior to departure

Dog sledding in Finland is a popular activity for tourists.

Dog sleds are typically cared for with great intention

Dogs and trainers prepare to depart on an early morning jaunt in the Arctic Circle

Dogs await their master's instructions

Dozens of shelters were constructed throughout the expansive camp

Fresh powdery snow clings easily to the tree trunks and branches in Finland's forests in 2018

Majority of the canines possessed a friendly, approachable disposition, however, a few remained surly and aggressive

Cottages are seen along the train tracks deep in Norway

In Norway's mountain regions, there is not much to do but wait out the long, harsh winters

More snow tunnels can be seen in the background of this photograph (to the right)

Residences are seen in the far distance (in Norway)

Muscular, hearty canines seem to enjoy the wintry conditions in the Arctic Circle

Norway's mountainous regions are primarily less distinct when compared to those in Switzerland

Preparing for departure into the Arctic Circle early on a February morning

Residences are enveloped by huge snowdrifts in Norway

Shot taken from the window of the train in Norway's mountain region

Snow enthusiasts arrive at a holiday resort in Norway

Snow fences are a common sight in Norway

Snowdrifts accumulated to the side of the building in Norway

Snow tunnels are constructed throughout Norway's mountainous regions

Teams comprised of six canines are what a typical dog sled ride consists of in Finland

The building where the author and several others enjoyed hot cinnamon tea and cookies after their journey through the forest

The camp was vast and consisted of many acres deep within the Finnish forest

The canines stayed the course for majority of the time, however, they were prone to veer off course on occasion

The canines were easily distracted by the most minute objects

Two canines enjoy a brief respite from the intense, grueling run

Two individuals wade through waist deep snow in Norway

The still, early morning air is positively exhilarating in remote regions of Finland

Snow machines are used to track the dogsleds

White was the fashionable color throughout Finland, Norway, Switzerland, Iceland, and Sweden in February 2018

Yellow (and red) buildings are quite commonly seen in Norway

Wood is a valuable commodity at the dog sled camp in Finland; the staff uses it for their camp fires

CHAPTER 14
DOCILE REINDEER AND ICE HOTELS

Having enjoyed my Husky safari, I figured I would find a reindeer ride fascinating and enjoyable as well—after I had warmed myself a bit from the stinging outdoor temperatures. As mentioned in the previous chapter, there were several reindeer farms along the dogsled route which traversed through the forests.

I explained to the driver of our bus that I would like to visit a reindeer farm yet, instead of joining the rest of the tourists which were eager to return to the city.

"This will be no problem," the bus driver assured me. "But I cannot take you there. I will find someone who can."

A few minutes later, after having made a few calls on his mobile phone on my behalf, the driver explained to me that one of his friends will arrive shortly to take me to the reindeer farm. I thanked him and waited for twenty minutes or so inside the cabin until my driver arrived.

Reindeer are a quite common sight here in Lapland, however, modern inventions such as snowmobiles and ATVs have largely replaced the need for any locals here to hitch a reindeer to a sleigh to transport items across the frozen arctic.

"Many decades ago, people here in Lapland relied on reindeer for transportation and distribution of items," my driver explained as we traveled on the snow packed roads along our route to the reindeer farm. "But today, most people have a snowmobile. It is much faster. Plus, there are now more roads and trails then there once were," he added.

Reindeer are quite clumsy and adorable creatures, and I tried to imagine traveling even a short distance with one. However, once I sat in the sleigh, it was obvious that they possess the capacity to do a bit of running. Still, the reindeer which transported me that day was not about to win any medals for sprinting anytime soon.

The steady clip-clop of their heavy hooves was fascinating, as their feet pushed the snow to the side with each step they took. We took a short loop around the reindeer farm late that morning. At the edge of the property, a sign declared that we had officially visited the Arctic Circle.

The clumsy animals appeared quite docile and perhaps even a bit sleepy. Their heavy coats protected them from the biting winds of the arctic region. The guide who operated the sleigh that day explained that reindeer like to eat a lot, and sometimes need to be coaxed to walk briskly while they are hitched to the sleighs.

All this exercise and excitement in the wilderness had roused my appetite, and I decided that I might take a look at what an ice restaurant would be like. Yes, here in Finland, deep in the northern regions, I ate a light lunch at an eating establishment which had been entirely constructed from ice and snow.

Initially, it had seemed a little odd to walk into a restaurant which was made of snow and ice. I didn't quite trust it and imagined that the structure might cave in while I was underneath. However, once inside, it was obvious that it had been built rather securely. The roof, sides, and of course the floors, were comprised of packed snow and ice.

Before placing my order, I was directed to a seat at a table—which was also made entirely of ice. *This will be the first time that I eat lunch off a slab of ice*, I mused, a grin forcing its way.

As I glanced over the menu, wrestling it between my gloved hands, I settled for a cheeseburger. The waiter took my order, walked outside the ice structure to a different building where the food was prepared, and then returned approximately fifteen minutes later with my food. (No food is prepared inside the ice restaurant).

The burger arrived nice and hot, a welcome respite from all the cold air which my lungs had been inhaling for majority of the morning. However, because the temperature inside the ice restaurant was around twenty-two degrees Fahrenheit, the burger chilled very quickly. I removed the gloves from my hands, in efforts of improving my grip on the food which I was about to eat. (It was nearly impossible to eat French fries with gloves on—I tried).

However, immediately upon removing my gloves, my fingers got really cold. You can imagine that this was not a meal which I chose to eat at a leisure pace. On the contrary, I tried to eat as fast as I could so that I could wear my gloves again.

It really was quite strange eating from a table which was constructed from a thick slab of ice. It was perhaps equally as unusual to sit on a chair made of ice, with only reindeer hide placed atop the seat of the chair to keep the initial cold from seeping too quickly into your bones.

Each year after the warm spring breezes usher in warmer weather and the heat of the sun intensifies, this ice restaurant, which was constructed with such creativity, melts to the ground. "Each year, around late May, as warmer temperatures arrive here, what you see of this restaurant will begin to slowly and steadily melt. Within a few weeks, nothing will be left except several big puddles of melted snow and ice. The structure that you are sitting in now, was only built late last fall," the waiter explained when I inquired about the unique structure.

Seeing that I remained curious, he continued. "Every autumn, sometime around November or early December, ice sculptors from across the globe will fly here and stay here for several weeks while they reconstruct a brand-new restaurant. This is done every year. A new one is built every autumn, because during the spring and summer months, the structure melts entirely. The sculptors also design many ice sculptures which we display throughout the restaurant. When they are done with their work, they fly home to their countries, where they live."

He explained that the sculptors get paid attractive wages. "We want very talented people to design and create the restaurant and its sculptures, therefore the manager of this property pays them well."

The property was a large resort area located in the wilderness of northern Finland. An ice hotel was also located on the property. This structure was also designed by a talented team of sculptors from all over the world. After I left the restaurant, I walked over to the ice hotel, which resembled a very large igloo.

Here at the ice hotel, hearty guests could choose to sleep in an igloo, for a pricey penny, of course. The hotel only operates throughout the winter months, due to it also being subjected to melting during the summer months. A different ice hotel is also built here each autumn.

Constructing these intricate buildings requires immense talent and effort, and regarding the small window in which the owners of the hotel could remain operational—due to warm spring temperatures—I understood the exorbitant prices which they charged per guest each night. At the front desk, which was carved from a large slab of ice, I inquired if there was any vacancy for that night. There wasn't, however, the manager told me that none of the rooms were occupied during that immediate time, therefore, I could take a look at each of the rooms if I wanted to.

The ice hotel consisted of several spacious rooms which had been carved from packed snow and ice. The property was small and could only accommodate a dozen guests. Each bed—most of them merely slabs of ice—were covered with heavy reindeer and/or bear hides. Additionally, heavy insulated sleeping bags were included in the nightly price for each guest.

Several hundred dollars were required to reserve a room here for one night at the ice hotel. Since they were booked to capacity that night, I was spared the temptation of sleeping in an igloo. The thought had greatly appealed to me. "People like the experience," the manager assured me, when I inquired about the levels of comfort throughout the night.

Later that afternoon, my driver took me back to the city. As I walked into my heated hotel room, I was reminded of how much I would have struggled if I had chosen to sleep in a twenty-degree room encased in ice and snow.

The long polar nights in the arctic regions can be quite beautiful, I learned, as I gazed out the window later that evening. The moon was casting its silver bands of light across the snowy landscape. I clutched my blanket a little closer and drifted off to sleep. I would need to rest up for the following day, since I had a plane ride scheduled for Iceland, the final country on my itinerary.

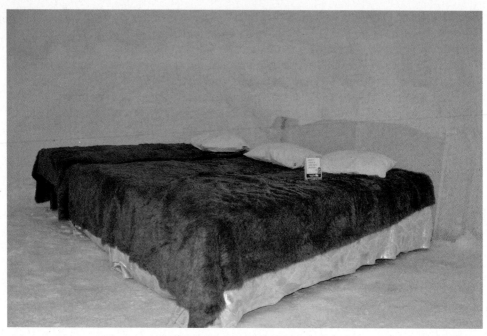

A bed consisting of ice blocks and wooden legs

A bitter cold enveloped the area

A bridge spans a Finnish river in proximity of the camp's orientation headquarters

A distant shot from the ice restaurant, ice hotel, and other shops in Finland

A distant shot of the forested area where the dog sled camp is located

A few reindeer await to trek through the forest with tourist-laden sleds

A sign post helps tourists orient themselves with their surroundings

A tall snowman welcomes tourists at the reindeer camp's entrance

A figure of a snowman is formed into the wall of the ice restaurant

A main building at the reindeer camp in Finland

Along the reindeer route in Finland

An exhausted reindeer poses patiently after a lengthy trek through the Finnish forest

Ice beds are a peculiarity in Finland

Fancy lodges such as this one offer tourists the luxury of warming themselves after enduring frigid rides through the snowy wilderness

Fresh snow clings to the roof of a posted sign in Finland

Lodges where some tourists choose to stay, instead of at the expensive ice hotel

Shot taken from the reindeer route

Snow fences were erected around the reindeer camp

Snow hung heavy on the branches at the Arctic Circle

Snow is piled higher than most buildings in remote regions throughout Finland

The entrance of the ice restaurant in remote Finland

The entrance to the restaurant is carved from an ice wall

The entrance to the ice hotel deep in Finland's wilderness

The reindeer path which is heavily traveled throughout the winter months in Finland

The main lodge in Finland, in proximity to the ice restaurant

While on a sled, transported by a reindeer and a trainer, in Finland

The sign announces the tourist's official arrival at the Arctic Circle

The temperature is displayed in Celsius in Finland

CHAPTER 15
ICELANDIC IMPRESSIONS

Prior to traveling to Europe, I had never expected that I would get the chance to visit Iceland. I was particularly pleased when I realized that it is easier to visit this country than what I had thought it would be. As I boarded my plane, I wondered what Iceland would be like once I arrived there a few hours later.

I find winter weather and snowy conditions more tolerable than some people do. However, I realized that once this wintry journey of mine had reached its conclusion, I would be ready for spring weather once again. Throughout the last several weeks, I had mostly seen snow covered ground, except, of course, in warmer regions such as Italy and France.

You may have noticed by now that I haven't been writing about every country that I visited during my journey to Europe. For example, since I merely traveled through a few of these countries as a passenger on a train, I didn't really feel as if I had much to say regarding those specific countries.

The countries which I observed primarily from the windows of my passing trains were; Lichtenstein, Austria, and Slovakia. I was aware at the genesis of my journey, that it would be impossible to visit every European country that I wished to, within my time frame. Therefore, I made a list of the ones which I felt I couldn't compromise on simply viewing from a train.

Trains were my primary mode of transportation while I was in Europe. I also utilized the convenience of a taxi on occasion, and I walked many miles, often choosing to explore the surrounding cities and sights on foot, whenever weather permitted me to do so.

The following list of countries were visited by stepping outside the train and either staying within each respective country for a day (or several), as my itinerary permitted. Spain, France, Belgium, Germany, Italy, Switzerland, Czech Republic, Hungary, Poland, The Netherlands, United Kingdom, Denmark, Sweden, Norway,

Finland, and last but certainly not least, Iceland.

As a bonus, I saw the country of Greenland quite well since we seemingly flew rather low across parts of the country, which provided an exceptionally unforgettable view of the valleys which were filled with snow drifts between the mountain ranges. From the windows of the plane, judging by the height of the mountains, it looked as if the snow drifts could easily be thirty feet deep in some areas. Perhaps it was not snow drifts which I saw, but glaciers, since glaciers cover approximately eighty percent of Greenland.

Iceland was the only country which I traveled to throughout Europe that did not possess even one mile of railroad tracks. I thoroughly enjoyed my time riding the rails and it was bittersweet to bid farewell to the last train that I had occupied in Europe. Traveling by rail had been so seamless here in Europe.

My thirty-three-day journey by train, taxi, bus, and planes was quickly reaching its conclusion. This was fully realized as I boarded the plane for Iceland, the last leg of the journey. The solo journey proved to be quite eventful, and one which I hope will never be erased from my memory.

Throughout the journey, I had spent more than one-hundred-fifty-two collective hours in a train car. I also traveled more than ten thousand miles on dozens of trains, with the combined total mileage which I traveled via train, plane, and taxi, and walking, culminating at slightly more than twenty-one-thousand miles.

Many friends were made along the way while I visited more than thirty cities, majority of them capital cities. Although the cities were interesting—for the greater part—I most enjoyed my time on the train, traveling through wilderness regions and farming communities.

Visiting the Land of Fire and Ice (Iceland) was memorable, for sure. The windswept, frigid country has a considerable amount of geothermal activity and, if I understood correctly, also currently has volcanic activity. The country is among the list of windiest countries on earth. I feel as if I can attest to this, since strong, bitter winds raced across the island for the duration of my visit.

Iceland is also full of visual surprises, but primarily resembles an eerie, moonscape atmosphere. Mounds of black rocks prevail and weave a jagged line across the horizon. The portion of the island that I saw was quite flat, with large snow-covered cliffs looming within the far distance, in proximity to the mountain ranges.

Taking advantage of the nearly perfect location of the guest house that I was staying at, I chose to explore regions of the island on foot for several hours. The coastline featured rippling, chilly waters, where waves crashed into each other. While standing atop one of the few sizable ridges, I gazed at the distant beauty of the snowy cliffs which surrounded the far edges of the waters.

The afternoon sun was fading fast, and before I was ready to leave, it became apparent that the daylight wouldn't wait for me. I hurried back to the guesthouse, approximately half-a-mile away at this point, and spent the remainder of the evening chatting with the owners of the guesthouse. The guesthouse was owned and operated by a local family, and they seemed quite interested in learning what life is like in the

United States. I, in turn, was equally fascinated by the stories they shared regarding life in Iceland.

One thing which I quickly noticed was that everything in Iceland seemed to be at least twice as expensive when compared to items sold within the United States. The prices were, in most cases, exceptional here. For example, a gallon of gasoline cost approximately $7.60 USD. However, don't allow the high prices to scare you; the Icelandic people compensate for their outlandish prices with exceptional hospitality. I truly felt like family while staying at the small guesthouse on the final night that I spent in Europe.

The following day, I explored the island with greater intensity. I rented a small car and set out to drive around the island. I was pressed for time, since my departure flight for the United States was scheduled to leave at three o'clock in the afternoon. That day, I didn't stop to eat lunch anywhere, I just wanted to see as much of the island as time permitted.

Hardly any motorists were on the roads during the early morning hours, and it seemed as if I had the beauty of the island all to myself. I watched the sun rise above the island, its deep colors painting the sky like a paintbrush.

With only two hours to spare before my flight departed, I returned the rental vehicle and hired a driver to transport me to the airport.

This solo journey of mine had unfolded quite nicely; much better than I could have envisioned at the beginning of the journey, when I had arrived in Spain a few weeks earlier, rather lonely due to the language barrier. There, I had tried to communicate with people, but it seemed more often than not, that they found the English language to be a perplexing one, and I, likewise, found the language in which they spoke, to be challenging.

Throughout the weeks, it had all worked out in the end, even though there were communication barriers on occasion, and numerous missed departures regarding my misinterpretation of the train schedules and the complex labyrinth of platforms. The journey was, I felt, a valuable learning experience for me.

People travel for many different reasons. I would say that I enjoy traveling internationally because of my insatiable curiosity regarding different cultures. It is rewarding to see how differently some people live. Also, while traveling, unknown adventures usually await around each corner.

Since returning home from my European excursions which I embarked on during the winter of 2018, I have had the opportunity of seeing a few more countries since then. Sometimes, upon arrival in a strange country, I am certain that I have placed myself in a situation in which I will regret considerably. There were a few times in which I initially felt that way upon stepping foot in exceptionally poor, undeveloped countries. However, too often, I discover that no matter how intensely the vast culture differences threaten to stretch me, a little stretching is good for the body and mind.

Here in Europe, the cultures were not so vastly different than that of our own within the United States. Even so, I felt that no matter how descriptive I would be, there are things which I saw, experiences which I had, emotions that I felt, which I couldn't fully describe to a reader. Seeing such things with one's own eyes is usually the best way in which to absorb and make sense of, any unfamiliar situation or unique region of the world. But within this book, as always, I set out to try my best—with words—of providing a picture within your mind's eye, of what it was like for me to travel solo throughout Europe.

The sign which announces the official arrival to the cold, European country

A few factories were seen throughout regions of Iceland

A landmark at the entrance of a national park in Iceland

A village in Iceland basks in the rare, low rays of a noonday sun

Aging buildings which were once used in Iceland's fishing industry, now stand idle

A lighthouse on Iceland's coastal region

A retired boat provides an opportunity to take an iconic shot as the winter moon rises in the distance

In the distance, the town of Keflavik can be seen

Boats are docked in the bay near Keflavik, Iceland

Barren, rocky terrain dominated the landscape in Iceland

Image made along a road which was located within a national park, in Iceland

Mountain ranges seemed to surround majority of the island

The author hiked off the roads quite a few times to explore the terrain more effectively

Buildings are also predominantly colorful in Iceland

One of the few churches in Iceland

Mountain ranges protrude into the cold winter skies in Iceland

Small houses were a common sight throughout the island

An Icelandic residence is seen in the distance under bleak winter skies

An Icelandic pony pauses for its portrait

Black, volcanic sand covers majority of the beaches in Iceland

Black, volcanic soil is seen here along a marshy area

The island has an abundant share of black soil, especially along bodies of water

The ponies are provided with a windbreak here

Throughout the summer months, the Icelandic meadows turn verdant and green

The town of Keflavik, up close

The bleak winter skies appeared to bleed into the frigid Icelandic water

Ponies enjoy munching on hay during an Icelandic winter

Soft, snowcapped ridges wrap around the mouth of the restless Icelandic waters

Random rock formations abounded throughout Iceland

Steam floats in the sharp winter breezes as it emerges from geothermal pipes

The Blue Lagoon, in Iceland

The entrance to a national park, in Iceland

The Icelandic landscape resembled that of an otherworldly atmosphere

A bird glides across the waters in Iceland as dusk beckons

A building along the coast, in proximity to Keflavik, Iceland

The warm waters of the Blue Lagoon, in Iceland

Vast strips of barren land prevailed throughout Iceland

The colorful hues of the morning sun remained visible for more than four hours

The snow covered roads were primarily deserted, except for the occasional delivery trucks headed to connecting towns and villages

The island had several lighthouses along the coasts

The longest sunrise that the author witnessed in his life, lasted for hours

The sun seemed to never quite make it up into the sky, even at midday

The vivid colors of the Icelandic sunrise remained vibrant for several hours

The small car which the author used to trek across the barren Icelandic regions

"For he shall give his angels charge over thee,
to keep thee in all thy ways."

Psalms 91:11 (KJV)

Previously released book by the author Leroy Martin, *Around the World in 37 Days.*

Nothing could prepare me for all that I was about to witness. Sure, I could immerse my mind in a thousand books composed by great travel writers. Or listen to a hundred lectures from a sea of articulate orators. If that all failed, I could certainly watch endless hours of slides and videos teaching of cultural disparity. However, none of these platforms would ever truly be adequate in preparing the eyes and mind of a pampered, sheltered American. At least, not for me. It simply had to be seen with my own eyes for any of it to have made any sense.

My travel partner and nephew Jeffrey Martin and I were told by several well-meaning individuals that traveling across dozens of time zones will be exhausting. They did not lie. It was. But if we were to break through the travel weary haze which was so intense it seemed to occasionally hinder our eyesight, and if we were completely honest with ourselves, we would tell you it was all worth it. Because it really was.

— *Leroy Martin*

While reading this book, I found it very interesting to learn of the many ways in which people make their living who have a lot less than we Americans. Floating farm markets on the Mekong River, where the buyer and seller would conduct their transactions from their small boats. Repairing garments while sitting at a sewing machine beside the road. Using hand cranked, smoky generators to make espressos, to training camels for racing in the Dubai desert, is naming a few. Speaking of camel racing takes us to the glistening city of Dubai where we ride the elevator to the top of the world's tallest building. The excessive lifestyles which Dubai offers the rich tourists is a stark contrast from the poor people living within Southeast Asia. We learn that, despite the struggles of the poor to make a living, they still have a smile to share with a stranger. I find that there is much to learn from other humans around the world and lest we forget, let's remember that God created every one of them.

— *Lavern Martin*

484-901-9671 or Email: atw37book@yahoo.com